The Termite Report

THE TERMITE REPORT

A Guide for Homeowners & Home Buyers
on Structural Pest Control

Donald V. Pearman

Pear Publishing
1224 Lincoln Ave.
Alameda, California
1988

Library of Congress Catalog Card Number: 87-90653
ISBN 0-943743-00-1

Printed in the United States of America

Typesetter: Design & Type
Printer: Graphic Arts Center

Contents

Acknowledgements

In the ten years since The Termite Report was conceived, many people have contributed their talents and special knowledge to this book. They all have my gratitude.

The text has been refined by the skills of many people. George McKechnie, Ph.D. helped to research and write the first nine chapters. Dawn Cunningham was the Editor and production coordinator. Toni Fricke edited the text and provided ideas and assistance on many of the details. Denis Kelly and Barbara Sokol also edited versions of the book. Elinor Lindheimer prepared the index.

The illustrations accompanying the text were drawn by Julie Glavin. The cover art was created by Donna Lariner, who also provided design advice. The final lay-out design was prepared by Keith Björkman.

Larry Butler and David Franklin gave inside information about the pest control industry. Dr. Wayne Wilcox provided information on fungi.

The book also received support in various ways from John Bacon, Faye Brehm, Jack Brenneman, Barbara Konecny, Rhoda Kroeger, John Pearson, Denise Roscoe, Jim and Irene Thesenvitz, and Peter Wohlfeiler.

Finally, additional thanks are due to the homeowners who shared their pest control experiences with me and allowed me to photograph their houses.

Author's Preface

The Termite Report is a product of years of contracting work; of professional advice from pest control operators, lawyers and state administrators; and of witnessing hundreds of cases of homeowners besieged by termite, beetle and fungus infestations.

I first stumbled into the pest control problem fifteen years ago as a real estate agent in the San Francisco Bay area. My work with homebuyers and sellers was affected by pest control work, yet the whole process of repair, extermination and certification was as much a mystery to me as it was to my clients.

A year later, I began working as a contractor on homes which were purchased with loans from the Federal Housing Administration and the Veteran's Administration. Initially, my bids only included electrical and plumbing repairs. Later, realtors began asking me to bid on structural pest repairs, using a pest control report filed by a licensed operator for reference. After I completed the repairs, an operator would inspect the house to certify it.

I was able to offer homeowners a package deal for all the repairs. My structural pest work cost 10 to 30 percent less than an operator's. Business thrived. Realtors brought me reports for a couple of houses a week. The more jobs I did, the more I realized that structural pest inspection is a wildly inconsistent profession. Often, the operator who inspected a house after my work was done would find problems missed by the first operator. I had to correct those problems at my expense. Some homes had so many missed infestations that those jobs didn't bring in a penny.

Eventually, I made a practice of checking over homes personally before making a bid on an operator's report. Seven out of 10 reports had missed enough damage that bidding on them was too great of a risk to take. Since I didn't have a pest control license, I couldn't repair damage that wasn't recorded on the first operator's report. If I didn't repair all the damage, the second operator might notice the unreported damage and deny the home a certification.

Pest control reporting seemed like a risky business to me—but it was worse for homeowners with no background in construction or home maintenance. So, 10 years ago, I channeled my thoughts and frustrations into a rough draft of this book.

Since then, I've photographed homes that make exemplary case studies of structural pest control. The book, meanwhile, underwent several revisions. I added researchers, editors, and illustrators to my crew. In 1988, we updated the book for the last time, and gave it the form you hold now.

I hope it helps.

The Termite Report

Chapter I

Pest Control: The Problem and the Cure

Among all the materials that people use to build dwellings, one dominates: wood.

Historically, people have used just about every kind of material that can be cut, mixed, or propped. Their ingenuity has produced leaf and branch shelters, mud huts, thatched cottages, brick buildings, and stucco bungalows. Whenever timber was plentiful, though, they've preferred to build shelters of wood.

Wood is relatively light and simple to handle and transport. It can be shaped easily by sawing, cutting, and planing. It can be assembled into almost any kind of structure. It's attractive and comes in many densities and grades for specific needs. It is a renewable resource and, until very recently, it was less expensive than other materials.

However, wood has one major drawback as a building material: it's organic. Like all other organic matter, it's subject to attack by various organisms that break it down and return it to the earth. As wood decays, so will the structure that is made from it. This may not matter much to a nomadic hunter throwing a few branches together to keep the family from spring rains—but if you plan to remain in the same house for ten, twenty or thirty years, beware of wood's enemies. They could be at work right now in the walls and beams of your home.

If you are a typical homeowner, your home—whether faced with stucco, brick, aluminum siding or shingle—is largely composed of wood. Most single family homes have an internal wood structure, no matter what material forms the outside surface. Just about every one of these homes is susceptible to the attack of wood-destroying organisms. Every homeowner, buyer or seller should become aware of the potential for structural pests to cause decay and destruction. Homeowners should learn to control pests by correcting defects in home design, maintaining vulnerable areas and repairing existing damage. Pest control shouldn't wait until a home is sold, the roof collapses or swarms of termites suddenly appear.

Help for the homeowner

A single family dwelling is a dream-come-true and an important investment for increasing numbers of Americans. As the cost of real estate rises, a greater part of their financial worth is invested in homes. The future value of this investment depends upon each home's structural integrity. If you plan to buy or sell a home, you should know its condition—especially with respect to structural pest damage and maintenance. You should know how to order, read, and interpret a structural pest control report, commonly referred to as a "termite report". You must be able to make your own judgement about the structural soundness and design of a home before you can buy or sell intelligently.

At first glance, the pest control report and accompanying repair estimate can be mystifying. This book will remove the mystery of pest control and open your eyes to the real nature of the house you are buying, selling, or calling "home."

"Read" your own home

Each home, no matter what the design, presents a unique set of structural problems with specific solutions. The design of the home, its age, basic

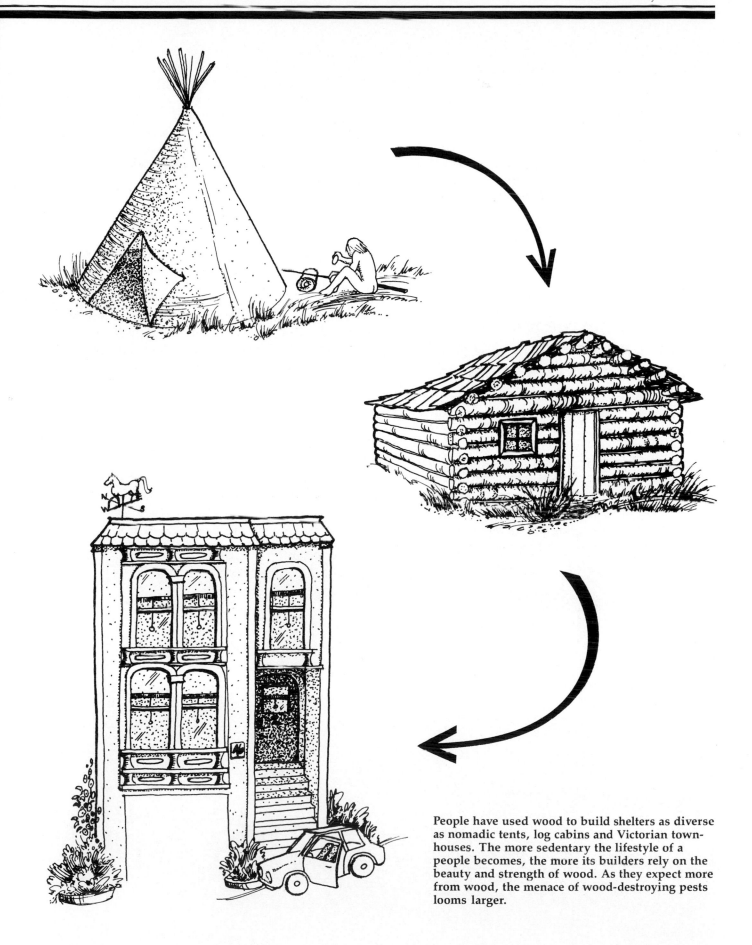

People have used wood to build shelters as diverse as nomadic tents, log cabins and Victorian townhouses. The more sedentary the lifestyle of a people becomes, the more its builders rely on the beauty and strength of wood. As they expect more from wood, the menace of wood-destroying pests looms larger.

building materials, geographical location, climate, grade, water sources and run-off, the type of drainage, gutters, roofing materials and more enter into the question of pest control.

This book enables you to "read" your own home from the perspective of structural pest control. It describes most of the pests that cause your home to decay and gives you information about the risks and benefits of various methods of controlling these pests. You'll get an insider's view of the standard (and sometimes substandard) termite report and advice for selecting and evaluating the pest control operator who provides the report. In short, this book shows you how to protect your most important possession: your home.

The allies: pest control operators, real estate agents and government agencies

Many homeowners are unaware that structural pests share their house until a pest control operator or real estate agent points out the damage. Operators and agents can be strong allies against structural pests if homeowners know the standard practices of these professionals. They can help you devise strategies for protecting your home against infestation or help you choose one that is a sound investment. Chapter 3 describes the options presented by operators and agents.

Government agencies provide another source of information about structural pest control. In some states, agencies have been set up to protect you from the few incompetent and possibly fraudulent operators and agents. You'll find a list of these agencies in Appendix 2.

Who are the enemies?

Termites, beetles, fungi and other wood-destroying structural pests have been around for several hundred million years. Termites, for example, evolved about 250 million years ago. Since that time, they have acquired some persistent survival skills. A termite can live upwards of 25 to 30 years and can burrow 25 feet or more underground. Humans, by comparison, are newcomers who appeared a mere 10 million years ago. From the pests' point-of-view, we arrived on the scene to provide a feast of tasty wooden structures.

Termites, beetles and fungi play a valuable role in the ecology of the forest by helping break down dead logs and branches to earth-enriching mulch. When people build permanent (or semi-permanent) wooden structures, these three wood-loving organ-

The view of an average home that welcomes visitors—the front porch—isn't always what it seems at first sight . . .

Improperly sealed and caulked cracks can encourage fungus decay underneath. A porch as decayed as this one could collapse under a child's weight.

isms become pests. Infestations have reached epidemic proportions with the growth of cities in the United States and other industrialized countries.

The pest we hear about most often is the omnipresent termite—a small, ant-like, social insect that feeds on cellulose in wood. Occurring in three forms—drywood, dampwood and subterranean—the termite inhabits almost every area of the United States. It attacks and destroys wood whenever it gets the chance. Chapter 4 shows you how to identify the different types of termites and how to recognize structural problems that can lead to infestation. It also describes the best methods of prevention and cure of termite infestation.

Another widespread structural pest is fungus, sometimes known as dry rot or wet rot. This organism attacks wood that becomes wet from leaks, inadequate ventilation or improper home design. Any wood with a moisture content of more than 20 percent—this feels wet to the touch—is susceptible to this pest. Chapters 4 and 5 show you how to prevent the conditions that bring about fungus growth.

Wood-destroying beetles bore through wood and weaken support beams, floors, joists, etc. Various species flourish in different climates and sections of the United States. The damage they do is serious and economically significant. Certain varieties, for example, can be introduced into your home through old furniture or firewood and then attack hardwood floors, solid furniture, and the structural elements of your house. Chapter 4 describes the various species and tells you how to recognize their presence. Treatments vary with species and with the extent of infestation.

What can you do about structural pests?

Once you understand the enemies' habits and methods of invading structures, get to know the design flaws and environmental conditions peculiar to your house. Chapter 5 contains checklists that guide you through, below and above your home (or would-be-home) to evaluate its potential for pest damage. This won't make you an instant expert, but it can help you become an active party in pest control decisions. In addition, you'll gain a first-hand understanding of professional termite reports.

The termite report: How to read it and what to do about it

The termite report, unfortunately, is often a cryptic mess of codes and sketches rather than an informative contract between operators, agents, buyers and sellers. Chapter 6 examines a typical report. It explains the pest control inspector's notations on pest damage, recommendations for repair, and tells you how to judge the dependability of the report.

Buying or selling a home

One of the most important, and sometimes confusing, elements in buying or selling a home is the responsibility of the seller to the buyer regarding the home's structural integrity and freedom from pest infestation and damage. It is crucial that both parties know exactly what these responsibilities and conditions are. Some buyers prefer the "as is" home—that is, a home sold with the understanding that any needed pest control work is the responsibility of the buyer, not the seller. Other buyers want all the problems cleaned up before moving in. Chapter 7 explains the definition of the "as is" home and gives you the pros and cons of buying or selling a home "as is." At times, the "as is" sale is advantageous to both the buyer and the seller. More often, as many realtors have found, one can buy plenty of trouble.

Pesticides: When and how to use them

One of the most vexing issues facing a homeowner who discovers an infestation is the use of pesticides. What are the risks involved? How can

When the owners of this 1920s cottage decided to sell it, a pest control inspection revealed $2,100 worth of fungus damage—even though the home had received a pest control clearance when the owners bought it three years before. It appears that the inspector who provided the clearance missed a lot of damage. It's unlikely that so much damage could have developed in just three years. Had the owners known how to "read" their prospective home and the original report, they could have called another company for a second opinion on the soundness of the house. Or if the couple had their home reinspected within two years by the original company, they could have held the company responsible for repairing the belatedly discovered damage. They could have saved themselves the expense of repairs neglected by the original operator.

you evaluate them? Do you have to use what the pest control operator advises, or are there other choices? All of these questions are discussed in Chapter 8. It will acquaint you with the substances used to control and eradicate wood-destroying pests so that you can make a decision based on knowledge of their properties and possible side effects. Don't place the well-being of a home before that of its inhabitants. Instead, consider the options that preserve the safety of those who dwell in the home.

Consumer complaints

While most pest control operators and real estate agents are fair, knowledgeable and honest, the prospective buyer or seller is occasionally victimized by an unscrupulous, incompetent or fraudulent operator who could cause serious harm. Chapter 9 outlines the criteria consumers may use to judge operators and to protect themselves and their homes from fraud and incompetence.

Improving the condition of your home

You can save yourself from some of the trouble and expense of structural pest control by keeping your home well-maintained. If you have basic carpentry and plumbing skills, you can probably do some simple structural repairs. Chapter 10 shows you how to cap a foundation, pour a curb, replace a shower stall and rebolt a toilet.

Structural safety

Homeowners need structural pest control for many different reasons: to satisfy the demands of a lender or buyer; to get rid of unsightly damage; to halt the slow decay of a well-loved old home. Chapter 11 adds another argument to this list: safety from natural disaster, especially earthquakes. Homes damaged by pests are much more vulnerable to seismic destruction than homes that are structurally solid. You'll read here about ways of reinforcing your home against earthquakes.

Chapter 2

Understanding the Problem

Control of structural pests and repair of the damage they do is very big business. Americans spend about $1 billion each year to repair homes damaged by termites, fungi and other wood-destroying organisms. Infestations are discovered in about 2 million homes each year in the United States. In countless others, pests are working undetected. In still other homes, improper structural design coupled with inadequate maintenance may yet lead to infestation.

There are good reasons to believe that the extent of the structural pest problem will be much greater in the future. Many homes now standing were built before knowledge about structural pests began to affect architectural design. As these homes continue to age, their structural defects make them increasingly susceptible to infestation. In time, they may need major repairs. Moreover, during periods of inflation, many people defer normal maintenance (such as roof and gutter repairs) on their homes.

On the average, more than 50 percent of all the homes in the United States have structural pest problems that may be undetected.

This can lead to infestation and structural damage. At the same time, more infestations are discovered during inflationary times as homes frequently change hands. All of these factors ultimately combine to significantly increase the amount spent on repairing the damage caused by structural pests.

Homeowners in every state are susceptible to pest control problems—problems resulting from the growth of the pest control industry as well as the activity of structural pests. All too often, the consumer is at the mercy of inadequately informed real estate agents or technically-fixated pest control experts who rarely have the time or inclination to make their craft understandable to the lay person.

Friends in high places

Federal and state government has begun to respond to the growth of the pest control industry with an incomplete patchwork of agencies. Most of these agencies serve only in an advisory capacity to the public. At the federal level, agencies such as the Building Advisory Board, the Chemical Biological Coordination Center and the Agricultural Board (all part of the National Academy of Sciences' National Research Council) have funded and published scientific research on preventing and curing structural pest infestations. The Federal Housing Administration (FHA) and the Veteran's Administration (VA) issue building guidelines for protecting homes against termites and other wood-destroying organisms. In addition, both of these agencies usually require a structural pest control inspection before they guarantee low down-payment mortgage loans. In so doing, they help buyers identify homes that have few structural problems. The Occupational Safety and Health Administration (OSHA) and the Environmental Protection Agency (EPA) regulate hazardous chemicals used to spray or fumigate houses infested by wood-destroying pests.

A number of states have set up structural pest control boards. These regulate the way in which structural pest inspections are made and reported, and, to some extent, the way in which structural damage and threatening conditions are repaired. The California Structural Pest Control Act, first enacted in 1935, established a professional licensing board. This board restricts eligibility for inspection and repair work to licensed pest control operators and specifies what kinds of infestations and conditions must be included in the report. Other states have set up similar regulatory boards.

Local governments have limited jurisdiction over the problems of pest control. County and city health departments are concerned with general pests—cockroaches, mosquitos, rats, etc.—that serve as vectors of human diseases and thus directly threaten the health of the community. They seldom become involved in problems of structural pests, even though general pests are also associated with structural problems such as improper drainage, plumbing, etc.

Local building departments are responsible for interpreting and enforcing the Uniform Building Code or local variants of it. Although they have general jurisdiction over the structural soundness of buildings, they have little knowledge of the damage pests do or the conditions that precipitate an infestation. They are mainly concerned that repair work done on an infested home conforms to building codes. Since these codes don't always reflect contemporary thinking on how to design a pest-free home, they might not stop repair work from recreating the conditions that led to the infestation.

Structural Pest Control Inspection

Occasionally, long-established residents will see termites swarm or notice excessively cracked walls, sagging floors, discolorations or litter. Yet the discovery of infestations in this way is an exception. All too often, residents live in ignorance of infestations until they put their home on the market and learn that it needs to be inspected for structural pests. In most states, the structural pest inspection is not required by law. In California, for example, the Structural Pest Control Board regulates who may perform a structural pest inspection and how it must be performed, but it doesn't require that the inspection be performed when property changes hands. Instead, the inspection is required by the FHA, VA, and most lending institutions.

The structural pest report lists two types of problems: (1) actual structural damage caused by an infestation of fungi, termites or beetles, and (2) structural conditions such as excessive moisture, inadequate ventilation, direct contact between wood and earth, etc., which, if left uncorrected, may eventually lead to infestation and structural damage. It usually costs much less to eliminating pest-encouraging conditions before infestations develop than it does to repair the structural damage that results from an infestation. An alert inspector

Mother Nature sees no difference between wood lying in a forest and unprotected wood in your home. Both are part of a complex ecological cycle that needs to be understood in order to protect your investment from destruction.

seldom fails to find at least one condition in need of correction, and usually finds many more. In many cases, both actual damage and structural problems must be repaired in order to complete a real estate sale or receive a loan.

Whether you are a buyer, seller or long-time resident, the ordeal of living through the repair of an infested home can be made much less traumatic if you have access to basic information about what will happen, what it will cost, what the risks are of any pesticides used, what conditions will lead to damage if not corrected, etc. In the past, it was difficult for homeowners to get this sort of practical information. The whole enterprise was shrouded in mystery. Asking for this information in lay terms was as unthinkable as asking for detailed information on major surgery. Homeowners were often told, "Don't worry. It's all too complex for you to understand. We're the professionals. Trust us to take care of everything. We'll send you the bill." They fixed, you paid.

Although some of the procedures involved in controlling infestations, repairing damage and correcting conditions may be too complex for the average homeowner to perform, many are very simple. None of them, in any case, are too difficult to understand. You have the right to know what pest control is about. Pest control operators don't always agree among themselves on what needs to be done in a given situation—or on how much repairs will cost. You need to make decisions based on knowledge of your home and pest control options, rather than fear, anger, or frustration.

What can go wrong?

You can't make a home 100 percent safe from structural pests unless you build it entirely of inorganic materials, such as brick, concrete, metal or glass. Even if it were possible to build a comfortable home with these materials, the cost would be prohibitive.

For the most part, then, people are limited to wood construction. Since varieties of termites are found in every state and since virtually no wood is completely free of destructive fungus spores, who should we blame when infestation does occur? Mother Nature for her seemingly harsh ways? The architect for a design that invited problems? The builder who failed to see that subcontractors carried out their work according to plans? A former owner who either failed to keep gutters clean or piled dirt too high along one side of the home? The pest control operator who failed to identify potentially troublesome conditions when inspecting the home 10 years ago? The state, for failing to be sufficiently informed about the hazards of wood-destroying organisms?

In a sense, they can all be blamed a little. Careful attention at almost any point might have broken the chain of infestation and damage. Instead of laying blame, homeowners and buyers need to be aware of the potential for infestation and take steps to correct conditions that lead to it. How do we do this? Read on.

Chapter 3

Allies

Besides state and federal agencies, you can count pest control operators and real estate agents among your allies in structural pest control. This chapter describes their responsibilities in the identification and repair of structural pest damage.

Pest control operators

Pest control operators are usually independent contractors licensed by the states in which they operate to perform specific types of jobs. Many states require operators to pass an examination be-fore they can be licensed. Depending on the state, an operator's work may include the following: inspecting a home for evidence of infestation or conditions likely to encourage infestation; preparing a report summarizing the findings; making an itemized, written estimate of all repair and alteration work needed and any chemical treatments necessary; performing this work and treatment; and supplying a certificate indicating that the home is free of active structural pest infestations. In cases where states regulate and license only one or two of these tasks, pest control operators routinely perform most all of them without regulation.

Inspecting a home is more of an art than a science. Inspectors rely on their own experience rather than on standard formulas. As a result, inspectors vary in their detection of infestation in hidden areas, such as this substructure.

The customary charge for a structural pest inspection varies greatly from area to area. In California, which has some of the most rigid regulations for pest control operators in the United States, inspection of a single family dwelling usually costs less than $150. Given the amount of work that goes into the preparation of a typical report, the inspector's travel time to and from the home, and the potential liability that the operator assumes for improper inspections, this fee seems quite reasonable. Pest control operators certainly don't get rich making conscientious inspections and reports.

Most companies subsidize the inspection and report side of the pest control business with repair and treatment jobs. Because inspection work usually isn't profitable and because only one in four or five inspections leads to a repair contract, some operators may tend to rush through inspections. They may miss areas that need extensive work. In fairness to the operators, it must be pointed out that it's often difficult to assess the full extent of pest damage until a house has been opened up to remove damaged wood and install replacements. In order to cover any damage the inspector may have missed and permit the operator to run a profitable business, repair bids usually overestimate the cost of damage found during an inspection.

Operators are very much aware of the pressures of competition when they make inspections and repair bids. They know that homeowners want to spend as little as possible on structural pest repairs and they know that the operator whose bid is lowest will look—at first sight, at least—most appealing. Operators know that one way of lowering their bids is to omit infestations from their reports. They also know that a competitor may report what they miss and expose this unfair practice. Some operators may risk missing infestations to offer lower bids, while others may risk offering higher bids to cover the expenses of all necessary repairs. Many pest control operators prefer to work on homes needing minor repairs. Contractors make proportionately higher bids and profits and face fewer risks of financial liability than they do in cases with more serious problems. Clean, simple jobs have fewer costly surprises than do big, messy repairs.

From the consumer's point of view, the most frustrating aspect of evaluating bids for repair work is that almost every pest control company bids on its own report. This report may not agree with any other and may not adequately describe what needs to be done to the home. The bidding process would

Regulations don't require operators to probe finished surfaces. Nevertheless, many inspectors probe stucco siding when they suspect it conceals badly damaged wood. A well-placed hole can tell an experienced inspector a lot about the condition of a home.

be much simpler if all contractors had to bid from a single, accurate report. When the operator is both inspector and contractor, as is the case in California, the financial incentive of profitable repair jobs influences inspections and reports.

On the other hand, California state law protects consumers by requiring operators to complete all the work outlined in their reports and to certify that their reports are complete. If the initial report is inaccurate or incomplete, the operators are usually liable for the expense of additional work necessary to meet the requirements of the certification. Under these regulations, operators must perform work that is profitable enough to provide a form of self-insurance for potential liability.

In effect, we have an informal and erratic sort of liability insurance system. Some jobs must be profitable enough to provide a financial cushion to the operators for those occasional situations in which they may lose thousands of dollars. For small contractors, too many inadequate reports, too many bad jobs or too much price-cutting in bids can lead to bankruptcy or revocation of their operating licenses in a short period of time.

The system that insures the quality and uniformity of structural pest control reports obviously needs improvement. This will come as agencies develop more specific guidelines for inspections and reports and as the pest control industry isolates the inspection and report role of operators from the financial incentives and risks of repair work. If this separation is to work, the industry needs an insurance system to warrant the quality of inspections and reports in much the same way as title insurance companies warrant titles on property.

Until the industry accepts such reforms, the best that you can do to protect your financial interests is to order two or more reports. This strategy is especially advisable if you have an older home (built more than 20 years ago) or one with structural features that might hide infestations from inspectors—such as decks, exterior stairs and finished surfaces that hide wood. You should also order additional inspections if the first operator's report shows thousands of dollars of repairs.

Compare the findings of each operator you've chosen carefully. If you notice any discrepancies between the reports, ask the operators to explain their findings. Based on what they tell you and on what you know about the pressures they're under, choose the one that you trust most.

Choosing a contractor

In most states, contractors' knowledge about structural pest problems is acquired through apprenticeships with experienced pest control operators, directives from state agencies, information supplied by manufacturers of chemical pesticides and application equipment, and educational services provided by state or national professional associations. Operators in California are required to attend continuing education classes. In many other states, operators' stores of knowledge may be spotty, out-of-date or biased, unless they've made the effort to keep up with new developments in the field.

Not all operators have relevant training or experience with the particular problems presented by

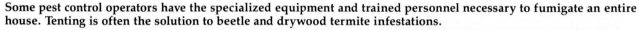

Some pest control operators have the specialized equipment and trained personnel necessary to fumigate an entire house. Tenting is often the solution to beetle and drywood termite infestations.

your home. Unusual construction details, soil or climatic conditions can stymie an otherwise competent contractor and result in an unsatisfactory job.

Pest control practices differ from contractor to contractor. Some businesses specialize in general pests (such as rats, cockroaches and ants) and others in structural pests (fungi, beetles, termites). Some companies have the equipment and specialized personnel to fumigate a home with an airtight tent and poisonous gas, while other companies limit their practice to spraying or brushing pesticides onto small areas. Some companies have the resources to tackle difficult structural repair jobs (such as those involving stair replacement, stucco or brickwork repairs, or extensive foundation repairs), while other companies must limit themselves to simpler jobs.

All these factors make the choice of a competent contractor very complex. In addition, it's often difficult for the consumer to obtain the kind of information that simplifies this choice. The most important factors to consider are the size of the company, its general business reputation and expertise in solving problems that your home may present, and its willingness to cooperate with you in what is almost always an unpleasant experience—living through pest control work.

Companies range in size from one-man operations to large national corporations. Some people believe small businesses tend to be more responsive, efficient and competitively priced than the larger contractors. Work is often supervised or performed by the owner of the business or by someone under the owner's direct supervision. Each customer accounts for a larger portion of the total volume of a small company's business than one would account for in larger companies.

On the other hand, larger businesses, even if they are slower and less competitive, may have greater financial assets. They may be better able to stand behind their reports and repair work should any claim be made by a consumer, without the threat of bankruptcy faced by smaller businesses. Big, well-known companies do enough business to be essentially self-insured. A legitimate complaint about work performed by a contractor may be more easily satisfied by a large company than by a small one.

With the complexities of the findings in a pest control report, its recommendations, and the inconvenience that repairs and pesticide application may cause you, it's very important to find a cooperative contractor. The operator should be able to explain the report, any inconveniences likely to be caused during repair and treatment work, changes in architectural details because of repairs (such as the inability to match an exotic stucco pattern or wood cornice) and potential health or safety hazards from pesticides. You and the contractor may need to reach compromises in scheduling the inspection, scheduling repairs so they don't disrupt your daily life, scheduling chemical treatments, and dealing with special considerations such as landscaping, pets or young children.

The most difficult information to gather when choosing a pest control operator concerns the company's business reputation. Try checking with the Better Business Bureau in your area or, better still, with the licensing board or agency in your state to find out if any complaints have been filed against the contractor and whether any disciplinary action was taken because of them. Remember that no contractor is perfect and consumer complaints are often without merit. The percentage of the contractor's customers that filed complaints is more important than the total number of complaints. Notice if there's a pattern in the complaints—a tendency, for example, for the operator to miss structural problems, to report that it's necessary to exclude certain areas of the house from inspection, to handle chemicals carelessly or to delay completion of the work. It may also be useful to talk to an experienced real estate agent for suggestions. However, it's probably best not to rely on a real estate agent to hire a company for you. Some agents may be tempted to select operators who make fast, superficial inspections and unrealistically low bids—which won't help you in the long run. Weigh the agent's advice against information from other sources and make the decision yourself.

Real estate agents

Real estate agents are seldom experts on termites or any other structural pests. They are often consulted about pest control operators, however, because structural pest inspections and repairs—usually performed when a house changes hands—may become part of the purchase contract. Agents aren't required to know about structural pests, but many are well versed in the structural pest control regulations pertinent to the transfer of property. Agents aren't required to know how to do repair work, but many have enough experience to direct you to the contractors that do the best work. Responsible agents learn all they can to protect the financial interests of their clients in a manner that is fair to both parties in the transaction.

In some states, real estate licensing boards or professional associations spell out agents' roles in pest control matters. California state law obligates agents to seek out and disclose all the facts about a property which are practical to ascertain—including structural problems. An agent who hides serious problems from a buyer or seller may be liable for any financial damage buyer or seller suffers once the problem is discovered.

A number of states prohibit real estate agents from recommending one specific pest control oper-

ator to clients. This is because a friendly business relationship between realtor and operator might conflict with the relationship between agent and client. A realtor's job is easiest when the structural pest control report looks good to both buyer and seller and the bid for repair work is low. An operator who finds much of his business through one realtor may oblige the realtor with quick, lenient inspections that make the condition of the house look better than it really is.

Ideally, an agent can help select an operator by giving the client a list of reputable companies with whom the agent has worked before. In practice, however, a real estate office usually has most of the

Many homes have details, like this corner decoration (photo, to left) and wood balustrade (photo, next page), that could be affected when structural elements beneath them need repair. Try to find an operator who is skilled in preserving and matching such detail.

Wood balustrade (carved support posts under railing.)

homes it sells inspected by a small number of pest control operators.

It's important to understand that three different interests affect the choice of an operator: those of the buyer, seller, and agent. A buyer wants a structurally sound home at the lowest price. The buyer wants an operator to make a thorough report, but a report listing many problems may frighten the buyer because it undermines confidence in the home's investment value. A buyer who purchases a home with many problems will want the problems solved by a competent (and maybe expensive) contractor before moving in. Since pest control repairs are usually paid for by the seller, the buyer may have little say in choosing the repair crew and may have to face moving in before repairs are completed.

The seller's preferences tend to be just the opposite of the buyer's. The seller wants the buyer to accept the home just as it is—after all, the seller has lived comfortably there for the past few years. Usually, the seller expects the operator to find little damage. If work is necessary, the seller wants it completed after moving out. If the first inspector makes a large repair estimate, the seller may arrange inspections by several companies and shop around for the lowest bid.

The agent's motive in choosing an operator is to get buyer and seller to agree on a sale with as little trouble and potential liability as possible. When a report identifies many problems, the buyer's agent will have to reassure the client that the home can be made as good as new and help the client re-evaluate the sales price. The seller's agent will have to smooth ruffled feathers and help the seller realize that the sale of the home may bring much less than originally expected. The whole deal may have to be renegotiated. With such a balancing act on their hands, even the vast majority of agents who conscientiously recommend the most professional operators may approach a pest control inspection with trepidation.

This house was sold 35 percent below market value because the seller didn't choose to repair infestations and structural defects. The following photographs show you some of the problems.

The roof leaked along the side of the house where you see a dip in the tar. Rainwater seeped down under the stucco siding and encouraged a fungus infestation in the corner.

This corroded heater flue in the substructure vented hot air into the air. Water seeping down the corner of the house helped increase the humidity in the substructure and hasten the spread of fungi.

White sheets of fungi grew where water condensed on the floor joists, significantly weakening the wood.

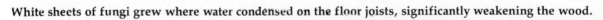

Chapter 4

The Major Structural Pests

The most common and destructive wood-destroying organisms are fungi, wood-boring beetles and termites. Left to themselves, any of these organisms could cause major structural damage to a wood-frame house. Several minor wood-destroying pests, including woodwasps and carpenter bees, aren't covered in this book. Although they can sometimes become a nuisance by causing cosmetic damage to finished wood surfaces, they are seldom responsible for structural damage.

Carpenter ants are also chiefly a cosmetic nuisance. They nest in wood already softened by decay and emerge to forage for food. These ants must emerge from their nests to forage, so homeowners usually catch infestations before long. Infested wood, riddled with slit-like openings called "windows", may be treated with insecticidal dust or spray. The most effective treatment is to create a barrier that prevents carpenter ants from entering the house. You can do this by cutting back tree branches that rest on the roof or by having an insecticide applied across the ants' trails. When an infestation is ignored, carpenter ants can spread into sound wood and cause expensive structural

Relative decay hazard faced by wood above ground in American homes:

Low; area tends to be dry

Moderate; area is moderately wet

High; area is among the wettest in the United States

Decay hazard may also vary within regions where differences in elevation affect climate.

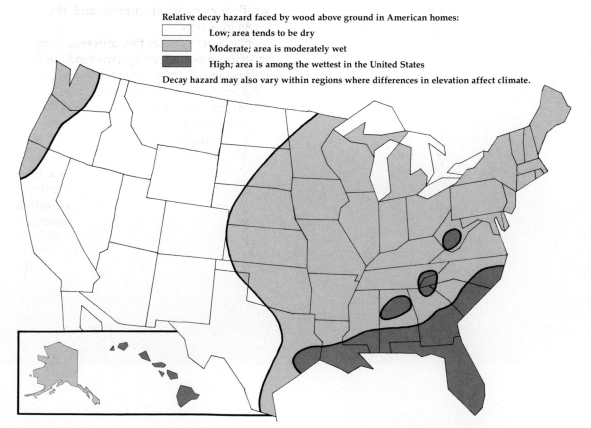

The same fungi that decompose tree stumps in the forest can be at work in the timbers of your home if there is a constant source of moisture.

damage. This problem is most common in vacation cabins and other structures uninhabited for long periods of time. Carpenter ant damage, however, is nowhere near as extensive as damage caused by fungi, beetles or termites.

Fungus Infection

The decay of wood because of fungus infection—commonly called rot—is an almost universal problem for homeowners. Fungus infections are triggered by excessive moisture in tropical and temperate, humid and desert regions. Fungi can survive temperatures from freezing to 110 degrees (higher temperatures kill them). In any climate, fungi thrive in wood that has become moist because of exposure to dripping water, seeping wet ground or condensation.

Fungus spores are present almost everywhere. It is a safe assumption that millions of such spores are present on the surface of the timbers of your home, just waiting for moisture conditions to trigger an attack. Although kiln-dried lumber is free from live spores when it leaves the kiln, it can be reinfected whenever it gets wet again.

Whenever wood feels damp to the touch (or when moisture content exceeds 20 percent), fungus spores begin to germinate. The fungus grows through the wood in microscopic, thread-like tubes that eventually form a white sheet on the surface called a "mycelium." As it grows, the fungus destroys the structural properties of the wood by secreting enzymes that turn wood cells into glucose, which the fungus uses as food. Pick up any piece of old wood that has been outside in damp weather and you'll see the results of fungus growth. The wood is light in weight and crumbly to the touch. It can literally fall apart in your hands. When you realize that a similar process may be weakening the wood in your home when high moisture conditions prevail, you begin to understand the dangers of fungus infection.

Wood decay takes two different forms—brown and white rot—caused by two kinds of fungi. At a certain stage of decay, you can see both kinds of rot on the surface of exposed wood. If wood is painted, decay fungi may cause the layer of paint to blister.

Brown-rot fungi secrete enzymes that destroy the carbohydrate material in wood, sapping it of strength very rapidly in the early stages of decay. Brown-rotted wood looks dark and is cracked across the grain into cubic pieces. It tends to shrink and collapse. Eventually, dried brown-rotted wood can be easily crumbled into a fine powder.

While all fungi need wood with moisture content above 20 percent to germinate, specialized kinds of brown-rot fungi can spread to dry wood by carrying water with them. Water-conducting fungi, as they are known, form root-like strands called "rhizomorphs" that conduct moisture to dry wood that surrounds infected areas. As long as water-conducting fungi have a source of moisture, they can infect an entire house. This kind of brown-rot is most prevalent in the southeastern and southwestern United States.

White-rot fungi secrete enzymes that destroy all material in the walls of wood cells. Wood loses strength gradually, but progressively, as decay proceeds. Wood with white rot looks bleached, with black zone lines bordering the bleached area. In the final stages of decay, the wood feels spongy.

Besides decay fungi, you may notice mold and stain fungi, algae, mosses and lichens on the surface of moist wood. These don't cause structural damage, but their presence signals that conditions are right for brown or white rot—and decay by these fungi may already be underway.

If a fungus infection is discovered in your home, there are several steps you can take to keep it from spreading. First, remove the source of the water that moistened the wood. Then remove the visibly decayed wood and the wood two feet beyond the damage. Replace it with wood that is pressure-treated with fungicide or that is naturally decay-resistant. Reduce humidity in the area, if possible, so the remaining wood will stay dry.

Though advanced decay leaves dramatic signs of its progress, most of the strength in wood is destroyed at such an early stage of infection that fungi cannot be detected by sight. Clearly, homeowners must correct conditions that lead to decay before they see its signs. Moisture builds up to decay-encouraging levels when wood touches damp soil or concrete (especially ground kept wet by poor irrigation drainage), absorbs water from leaking pipes, roofs or gutters, or collects condensation in poorly ventilated spaces. In some kinds of infection, fungi actually serve as a conduit of water from moist ground to otherwise dry wood.

Several techniques are used to prevent fungus decay. The most obvious and successful one is to keep wood dry. This requires:

1) adequate ventilation of the basement or crawlspace and inaccessible areas under stairways and enclosed stucco work;

2) proper drainage of surface water and roof runoff away from walls and foundations—via roof overhang, gutters, downspouts and grading at ground level.

3) use of moisture barriers on wood, including paint, to keep water away;

4) checking exterior wall surfaces for cracks—especially around windows, doors, and roof line;

5) checking the roof for leaks—especially around flashings (points where chimney,

Powderpost beetles, enlarged.

plumbing vents or other structures penetrate the roof line).

Adequate ventilation is especially important in insulated spaces. Insulation is an important part of energy conservation, but insulation that traps moisture vapor inside a house can inadvertently cause condensation in walls and ceilings. In particular, make sure that insulated basements are properly vented.

Some people brush or spray wood with preservatives such as copper naphthenate to protect it in areas of high humidity. Most experts do not believe this is effective because treating the surface of wood may not kill fungus spores inside. It's important to check moist wood for decay frequently and to reduce moisture as much as possible.

Wood used in the structural frame of a house (such as a mudsill) is often pressure-treated with an "arsenical" at the mill. Pressure treatment penetrates deep, but seldom through the entire cross-section of a wood piece—particularly in the case of hard-to-treat douglas fir. If you need to saw through pressure-treated wood, brush the cut end with copper naphthenate. Paint and other sealers help to reduce the penetration of water into wood. Sometimes the best solution is to build with redwood and cedar, which contain high concentrations of naturally-occurring fungus-resistant substances.

In order to eliminate sources of decay, it's difficult to overstate the importance of sound architectural design, intelligent placement of the home on the lot and careful attention to construction details. Above all, it's important to keep water away from the wood in your home.

Wood-destroying beetles

Three kinds of wood-destroying beetles are prevalent in the United States: the true powderpost beetle, the false powderpost beetle and the furniture beetle and its close relatives. During the larval stage of development all three beetles bore through timber, ingesting the wood and excreting a fine powdery substance, called "frass," into the channels they excavate. Wood attacked by wood-destroying beetles is often riddled with such channels, called "galleries," which run parallel to the wood grain. When struck with a solid object such as a screwdriver blade or the claw of a hammer, they release clouds of telltale frass from the exit holes, which are about one-sixteenth inch in diameter. Timber can be badly weakened by this infestation, even though the only signs of the beetle's work are the tiny exit holes through which adult beetles emerge. Beetles can reduce a sturdy beam to a hollow shell.

True powderpost beetles insert their cylindrical eggs into the surface pores of wood. After the eggs have hatched and the larvae matured, they bore just

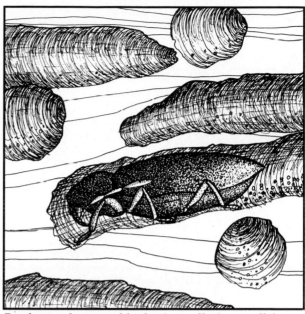

Beetles weaken wood by boring galleries parallel to the wood grain. In their wake, they leave debris called "frass."

The small holes in this beam were the only signs of a beetle infestation that hollowed the wood to a paper-thin shell. The extent of the infestation was discovered when an inspector's probe broke the beam open.

A swarm of winged termites departs its old home to found new colonies. Swarming is an uncommon sight inside homes and is a sign of advanced infestation.

below the surface of the wood to pupate. When adults emerge from the pupae stage, they bore through the surface, form an exit hole by pushing out some frass, find a mate and start the cycle again by depositing new eggs in the wood. The beetles will reinfest a board of wood with eggs until it no longer provides enough sustenance.

Adult powderpost beetles are about one-eighth inch long, reddish brown or black, and somewhat flattened-looking. They are seldom seen during the day, but at night they may be seen crawling on floors, window sills, and furniture. They usually infest hardwoods such as floors (especially floor elements that were not adequately heat-treated before installation), cabinets, tool handles, or other wood objects with a high carbohydrate content. They cannot digest cellulose. Because of the way they lay their eggs, true powderpost beetles prefer woods with large pores such as mahogany, oak or ash.

False powderpost beetles, unlike the "true" type, bore egg tunnels into wood to deposit eggs. The larvae attack wood in much the same way as the true variety, and emerge as adults after passing through the pupae stage. Adults are one-eighth to one inch long, dark brown or black, and cylindrical in shape with a very rough surface. They too are unable to digest cellulose, so they attack woods high in starch content—typically the sapwood of hardwoods, but sometimes softwoods. Their frass is coarser than that of the true variety, and may contain wood fragments. The false powderpost beetle is mainly found in the tropics, and isn't as serious a

pest in the United States as other wood-destroying beetles. The particular species of false powderpost beetle that does the most damage is the bamboo borer. True to its name, it infests furniture and other objects made of bamboo.

Furniture beetles breed not only in the cracks and crevices of old wood—especially dead, dry limbs and firewood—but also in structural timbers of a home and, of course, in furniture. The larvae burrow into wood, tunnel for about a year or so, pupate, then bore back through the surface and emerge as adults. They are one-third inch long, reddish-brown to black-brown and similar in shape to the false powderpost beetle, but with a smoother body surface. Unlike both powderpost beetles, furniture beetles are able to digest cellulose into nutrients they can metabolize. Furniture beetles often enter a house in infested firewood or antiques. Adults are often seen on window sills during the day because they are attracted to light.

In cases where true powderpost beetles have infested hardwood paneling or flooring, it is sometimes possible to treat the infestation with locally-applied pesticides. In most cases of beetle infestation, though, treatment requires tent fumigation of the entire structure with methyl bromide or other highly toxic vapors. Yet even the effectiveness of fumigation against beetles is limited. Beetles often leave their galleries before the damage is discovered, so treatment may come too late. Beetles can also reinfest wood shortly after fumigation. In any case, the timbers that have been structurally damaged should be replaced.

Termites

Termites are social insects. Their colonies include several different body forms, each of which is adapted to a different job. The reproductives (king, queen and replacements) produce soldiers that protect the colony from invasion and nymphs that can be changed to reproductives, soldiers or workers. Workers perform most of the work, including feeding all the non-workers. When the colony is at least two years old and ready to expand, and when environmental factors are right (often after the first spring or fall rain), a swarm of winged "alates"—mature males and females—makes a dispersal flight. When they find a favorable site, the swarmers lose their wings, pair off and begin a new colony. They mate, form a cell by boring into a choice piece of wood and begin producing young. It is during this brief swarm that homeowners may first notice the termites and begin to worry about their homes.

Three types of termites are common in the United States: subterranean, drywood and dampwood (or wetwood). Drywood and dampwood termites have a similar biology. These termites don't have a true worker caste, but produce nymphs that can be converted into false workers, soldiers or, if a king or queen weakens or dies, into reproductives. Subterranean termites, in contrast, have true workers that can become soldiers, but not nymphs or reproductives.

Drywood termites are found along the southernmost boundaries of the United States, including the southern parts of Georgia, Alabama, Mississippi, Louisiana, Texas and New Mexico; all of Florida and Arizona; and along the coastal regions of California and the Carolinas. Dampwood species are found in states west of the Rocky Mountains from British Colombia to Southern California (the rottenwood termite variety), in the southwestern states from Texas to California (the desert dampwood termite) and in Southeast Florida (Florida dampwood termite). Subterranean termites are found in all 48 continental states and in Hawaii.

The behavior and wood-destroying habits of these three types of termites are distinct. They tend to infest different parts of the home, show different signs of infestation, have different moisture needs and require different inspection and eradication techniques.

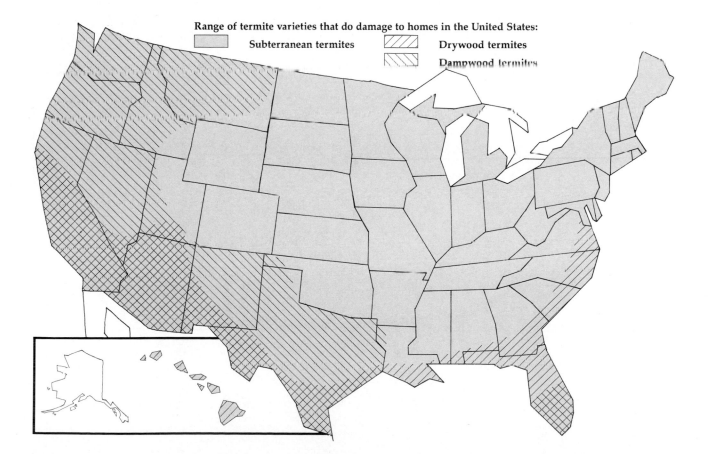

Range of termite varieties that do damage to homes in the United States:
Subterranean termites   Drywood termites   Dampwood termites

Subterranean termites live comfortably in large, earth-walled colonies under the substructure of a home. Workers build shelter tubes that reach above ground, over concrete slabs, towards mudsills, joists, and anything else made of untreated wood (1). They extract food from the wood and take it back to the queen, king, soldiers, and nymphs (2). When the colony outgrows its living quarters, winged alates emerge for a dispersal flight (3).

Subterranean termites. Subterranean termites cause the vast majority of termite damage in the United States. This is because they are more widely distributed than the other common termite forms and because they form large underground colonies (sometimes containing hundreds of thousands of members) which are very difficult to eradicate. Because their soft bodies lose water when exposed to dry air, this species must stay in close contact with the earth and its moisture. Above ground, they shield themselves from the drying effects of the sun and wind, against invasions by ants and other predators, and conceal themselves from the eye of the observer with brown shelter tubes. The tubes are made of excrement and other secretions mixed with particles of earth, sand or wood. Only subterranean termites build shelter tubes.

These termites move into a home by excavating galleries in wood that has contact with the earth, finding cracks in concrete through which they can pass protected and undetected, or building shelter tubes over concrete footings. The galleries they form in wood follow the soft portion of the annual rings and give heavily-infested wood the appearance of pages in a book.

Since subterranean termites approach a home from below, the point of infestation is almost always the substructure. Termites begin their attack at the mudsill, unless it's made of redwood or some other wood containing natural or applied preservatives. If it is, the shelter tubes bypass the mudsill and continue on to the closest untreated wood in the substructure. The tubes, however, are usually easy to spot and to break during an inspection, unless hidden inside cracked concrete foundations, under tongue and groove sheathing or other obscuring features.

Inspection for the presence of subterranean termites requires careful examination of the entire accessible substructure including, if possible, every inch of the mudsill and other exposed wood members. In addition to a visual inspection for shelter tubes or break-through holes, inspectors find clues about the condition of the wood by tapping it for a hollow sound or probing it with a screwdriver blade. This inspection is easy to make in homes with full basements and uncovered walls. In homes with crawl spaces—often no more than 12 inches high—inspectors must literally crawl along the entire perimeter of the home. Slab construction homes are the most difficult to evaluate because the mudsills are concealed. Here, the inspector must break a hole near the foundation to check for termites. Otherwise, there are no clues to make the inspector aware of these pests.

Treatment for subterranean termites varies greatly from case to case, depending on the extent of the infestation and the construction of the home in

This cross-section of a mudsill reveals the galleries in which subterranean termites live.

Subterranean termites can build tubes nearly a foot high in their attempts to reach wood. They make their way by detecting sources of heat, and are often seen near heaters.

question. Fumigation isn't effective because shelter tubes offer partial protection from gases. In addition, fumigation can only eradicate a small portion of a nest that may extend five to 10 feet underground. Instead, pest control operators typically use one or more of the following techniques: correction of all conditions likely to lead to termite infestation, especially earth-wood contact, wood embedded in concrete and faulty land grade; installation of a mechanical or chemical barrier between the earth and the wood structure; chemical treatment of the wood substructure; and chemical treatment of the foundation or the soil surrounding the foundation. The chemicals that operators apply against subterranean termites remain toxic for years after a treatment. The most popular termiticides are chlorpyrifos, an organophosphate chemical, and permethrin, a synthetic pyrethroid. Termiticides containing chlorinated hydrocarbons, such as chlordane, were once industry standards, but most have been banned because of their toxicity to people.

Drywood termites. Unlike subterranean termites and desert dampwood termites, drywood

termites don't require contact with soil or a constant moisture source in order to flourish. A male and female bore directly into the wood chosen for the nest, and excavate a sealed chamber where the queen lays her first eggs. These hatch into soldiers, which protect the colony from invading ants and other predators, and into nymphs which attack the wood to feed themselves, the soldiers, and the reproductives. Drywood termites form large chambers which cut across the grain of the wood, and connect these chambers with small tunnels. Fecal pellets excreted by the termites are placed in some of the spare chambers or kicked out of holes made in the wood specifically for that purpose. Piles of such pellets below kick-out holes are often the first sign of a drywood termite infestation.

Drywood colonies tend to be much smaller than subterranean colonies. A mature colony may contain several thousand members. Because the colonies are smaller, drywood termites tend to cause less severe damage to buildings than do subterranean termites. The colonies' small size and lack of need for a continuing supply of moisture, however, make it possible for these termites to be transported from one home to another in furniture and other wooden objects. Unchecked proliferation of multiple colonies can cause extensive infestation and damage. Southern California has been especially hard-hit by the drywood termite.

Drywood termites often enter a home through an attic vent, bore into a wood shingle roof, or crawl under the sheathing paper to attack roof sheathing. In hot, dry regions, they sometimes infest the substructure through a foundation vent or other hole. They attack sheathing and structural members in the attic or basement, and infest wooden window or door frames and furniture.

An inspector checking for drywood termites looks for kick-out holes, chinks and cracks in the wood surface, as well as telltale piles of wood debris and fecal pellets near them. In addition, the inspector looks for plugs which seal off entrance and exit holes. Tapping the wood for a hollow sound often helps locate galleries. A screwdriver probe confirms their presence.

Treatment for drywood termites is similar to that for beetle infestations—tent fumigation of the entire home with a toxic gas, usually methyl bromide. In cases where the infestation is limited to a small, accessible area, the operator may inject a toxic liquid or dust into the chambers. Any wood that has been structurally damaged should then be replaced with pressure-treated members.

Dampwood or wetwood termites. With one exception (the desert dampwood termite of the southwest), the dampwood termites don't require contact with the ground in order to infest a structure, as long as wood is continuously wet. They excavate wood in much the same way as drywood termites, but leave fecal pellets in all their chambers and tunnels (messy little fellows). The most common species of dampwood termites tend to be larger than their drywood or subterranean relatives and form smaller colonies.

Dampwood termite infestations frequently occur in forest and beach cabins, especially where lawn or garden irrigation keeps wood damp. Floors under leaking toilets and wet porches are especially vulnerable. Because dampwood termites tend to work systematically through a building from basement to attic, dampwood termites are capable of doing great damage to homes before they are detected. The point of entry can be anywhere along the exterior of a house, but continuing sources of moisture from garden watering, poor drainage, plumbing leaks or a creek or pond create the preferred conditions for entry.

Inspection for dampwood termites is similar to that for drywood termites. In addition, discovery of a continuing source of moisture sometimes reveals a dampwood infestation. Dampwood termites will leave once the wood is dried. Besides repairing structural damage caused by the termites, it may be necessary to replace timbers decayed by fungi.

Drywood termites enter an attic through openings such as vents without screens (1). They carve their chambers in rafters (2), sheathing, and other structural members.

Chapter 5

Problem Conditions: How to Check Your Home

Inspections can be an effective preventive measure against structural pest infestation when they are performed every one and one half years. Inspections can catch pest-encouraging conditions and incipient infestations before the financial expense of extensive repair and treatment is necessary. One home near San Francisco, California, for example, could have been spared $12,000 in repair work if its owners had ordered inspections regularly. Twelve years before the fungus damage in this house was discovered, the owners had the heater in the basement repaired. Unfortunately, the heater flue wasn't reconnected properly—three screws were missing. Warm air escaped from the heater into the substructure and the temperature there rose considerably. Since ventilation was poor, humidity also rose. These conditions encouraged fungus growth in the subfloor of the house. The problem was discovered when someone literally fell through the floor over the basement. If this home had been inspected regularly, however, the fungus-encouraging conditions could have been detected at the point when all the repairs needed were the three flue screws and the ventilation.

This improperly repaired heater caused $12,000 in structural damage. Three screws that should have connected the flue to the heater were not installed, allowing warm air to escape into the substructure.

Pest control inspections may seem expensive if you've never experienced termite problems before. Inspections add up to a paltry sum, though, when compared to the thousands of dollars you could spend on major structural repairs. This chapter shows you what operators look for during inspections and how regular inspections can save you from expensive repairs. You'll take a tour of the structure of your home from foundation to rooftop, following the footsteps of careful inspectors. You'll begin to "read" your home for conditions that invite infestation and structural damage and you'll learn what operators do to correct them. This tour will increase your literacy when it comes to reading a professional operator's structural pest control report.

You probably won't catch quite as many problems as a professional inspector would. Some types of home construction require more knowledge and experience than a consumer guide like this can summarize. Besides, you might not be ready to put on overalls and take to the crawlspace or the roof to probe for decay and infestation. Inspection can be strenuous and grimy work. In addition to structural pests, inspectors occasionally encounter snakes, poisonous spiders, rats and skunks in the crawlspace.

Because the ventilation in the substructure was poor, humidity rose.

Moisture condensed on the floor joists and eventually weakened them so much that a footstep above caused them to collapse.

The basic principles of disease-free home maintenance are quite simple: keep all wood in the structure of your home dry to the touch (moisture content below 20 percent) and make it as difficult as possible for invading organisms to get to the wood. The number of checkpoints in a home and the techniques for examining them, however, can be complex. To simplify them, this tour is divided into five stages that correspond to the basic structural areas in your home. For each stage, there is a checklist of potential problems and an explanation of each problem.

The inspection begins at ground level with an inspection of outside surfaces and surrounding ground. Then you may enter the basement or crawlspace (if any) to inspect the substructure. In the next stage, you'll examine the living areas and any attached structures such as a laundry room or garage. After that, enter the attic to look at the underside of the roof. Finally, you may climb a ladder to check the outside roof, gutters and leaders and upper parts of the exterior walls.

Exterior ground level

In this first stage, you'll make a slow circle around the outer perimeter of the house, checking for the problems listed below. You'll examine the intersection of the walls of your home and the ground, including the earth several feet out from the walls and the walls themselves as high as you can reach without a ladder. When you climb to the roof in the final stage of the tour, you can examine the highest areas of the exterior walls. Some of the inspection techniques described at this stage require you to relate what you see outside with what you see during the inspection of the basement or crawlspace (if your home has one). It may be useful to read through this section and the one on substructure before carrying on with the tour.

Checklist I: Exterior grade level

1) ☐ Evidence of infestation
2) ☐ Earth-wood contacts
3) ☐ Faulty grade
4) ☐ Drainage
5) ☐ Exterior plumbing leaks
6) ☐ Excessive moisture
7) ☐ Infested tree stumps
8) ☐ Formboards left in place
9) ☐ Additions without proper foundations
10) ☐ Planter boxes
11) ☐ Fences and posts
12) ☐ Abutments, columns, balusters
13) ☐ Exterior doors and jambs
14) ☐ Porches, balconies and landings

1) Evidence of infestation. Use what you've learned from Chapter 4 ("Major Structural Pests") to look for evidence of fungus, beetle or termite infestation.

Loose or blistering paint, water stains or decayed wood on exterior walls may indicate the presence of a fungus infection. Probe any suspicious-looking wood with your screwdriver. Sometimes you can see the fungus itself covering the wood and leading to sources of moisture.

Beetles make telltale pinholes in wood about one-sixteenth inch in diameter. Tap near any suspect holes with a solid metal object. If the holes release a cloud of fine sawdust or if the tap reveals a weak area in the wood, beetles may be at work.

Brown shelter tubes on the side of concrete foundations, along the exterior siding of the house, or inside cracks in stucco or other siding material are signs of subterranean termites. Dampwood termites might be found near moisture sources such as leaking faucets, outside showers or irrigated areas. Drywood termites seldom leave signs visible from the outside of the home.

2) Earth-wood contacts. Whenever wood—even wood such as redwood or cedar that contains natural preservatives—comes into direct contact with the earth, the chances of decay and termite infestation increase dramatically. Modern foundations are designed with about eight inches of concrete or other non-wood material between wood substructural members and the earth. This prevents surface water from being absorbed by the wood, and makes it more difficult for termites to reach wood.

Sometimes, substructural wood or siding contacts the earth directly. This situation may arise with the build-up of decayed vegetation around the house, soil erosion, or careless movement of soil during gardening or construction. In some areas, old homes were built directly on soil without the benefit of concrete or stone footings. Decay in these cases can only be arrested by installing foundations under the house.

Check any exterior wood (siding, substructure, porch, fence, or other abutment) for adequate clearance above the earth. Look for wood members, especially vertical ones, that are embedded in concrete, where dips and cracks might hold water. They should rest on concrete footings topped with redwood mudsills or treated douglas fir, which prevent moisture build-up.

If you find any structurally unnecessary wood touching the earth (such as wood piled under a deck), remove it. If you find that soil has built up high around the house, break the contact between earth and wood by removing soil to lower the earth grade level (see section on faulty grade below). Be careful about extensive digging. In some cases, removing soil can cause tipped foundations and drainage problems (see section on drainage below). You may need to install a higher concrete foundation over the existing one. This last procedure is known as raising or "capping" a foundation and is explained in detail in Chapter 10.

3) Faulty grade. This structural defect often leads to earth-wood contact and moisture build-up. "Grade" refers to the height of the ground in relation to the top of the foundation. The exterior grade includes all of the ground that extends four feet out from the walls of your house, whether the ground is earth, concrete (as it would be if a sidewalk or driveway comes up to the house) or another material. A "faulty grade" exists when the top of the foundation is even with or below the ground outside. You may need to inspect the substructure in order to determine whether your house has a faulty grade.

In bad cases, the exterior grade may even be higher than the mudsill. If your home has wood siding, you'll have a case of earth-wood contact on your hands. If the siding is of a non-wood material such as stucco, you'll still have problems with moisture as water seeps from the ground, through siding, into wood structural members.

If the grade around your home is faulty, you may need to lower the exterior grade or cap the existing foundation. If you cap the foundation, you should raise the top of the foundation six inches above the exterior grade. This satisfies the grade requirements of most local building departments.

4) Drainage. The general terrain of your home site, the earth grade level and the kind of foundation on which the structure rests determine how difficult it will be for you to drain ground moisture away from your home. Some home sites tend to collect runoff from a large area and direct it toward the foundation. Others are swampy because they lie in an area with a high water table, a spring or other underground water source. All of these conditions mean trouble. Even on otherwise perfect home sites, careless landscape grading or inadequate gutter downspouts can cause structural damage and infestations. Eventually, concrete footings under the house's perimeter may become waterlogged and begin to deteriorate; mudsills and other wooden substructural elements may become wet

The position of the walkway and the level of the garden encouraged water to run toward the foundation of this stucco home. In addition, the foundation was below grade. Much of the wood along the foundation had to be replaced and the foundation itself had to be capped.

Wood siding that touches the exterior grade absorbs moisture from the earth and decays. This siding is so decomposed that a screwdriver can poke through it to the mudsill (top). The mudsill, seen from the substructure, is also wet and decayed (bottom). The mudsill would have had a longer life if it was at the proper grade (at least six inches above the ground outside).

and start to decay; and soil erosion may undermine foundations.

Drainage problems are less critical for pole homes than for those with conventional foundations (such as perimeter footings). In pole homes, only the support posts contact the ground or concrete piers. Even so, posts and piers will last longer and face less danger of being loosened by erosion if your home site has adequate drainage.

To check drainage on your home site, run these simple tests:

a) Look for evidence of surface water (water stains or fungus growth) on the foundation and exterior walls. Water-soaked concrete foundations give off white lime powder which has been leached out by water. In time, the concrete becomes crumbly. It can no longer support the weight it was formulated for.

b) Check the earth grade with a water hose. The water should run away from the sides of the house for several feet.

c) Run water from a garden hose down rain gutters and downspouts to check for leaks or blockage. Make sure that the leaders end either in a drainage pipe that really does drain or above a splash block (which, in the long run, is safer than a pipe because it can't clog up).

The most important principle of home site drainage is to make the earth grade at the foundation of the home slightly higher than elsewhere. This allows surface water and water falling from the roof to drain away from the foundation. You might also try these strategies:

a) Install perforated drainage pipe in a ditch two feet below the level of the footings, cover with drainage gravel and building paper, then fill with earth to the existing grade.

b) Correct gutter and downspout problems, so that they no longer drain water near the foundation.

c) Repair any wood, concrete or other material damaged by surface water or resulting fungus infection.

5) Plumbing leaks. Dripping hose faucets and leaking sewer pipes keep foundations moist, encourage decay and provide a constant source of water for subterranean and dampwood termites. Dripping outside faucets will be obvious to you. Leaking sewer pipes make the earth above the leak cave-in slightly. Have the leaks repaired by a competent plumber and check the foundation and substructure near the leaks for damage and termite activity.

6) Excessive moisture. This term is used in the structural pest control industry to signify that moisture from several possible sources has collected to the point that the humidity level can trigger a fungus infection. Possible sources include the four conditions listed above. Other examples of moisture sources are: heavy vegetation (such as ivy growing on the north wall of a home) that prevents siding from drying sufficiently after rains; a natural spring in an unexcavated area of the basement; condensation on interior plumbing pipes; and water from kitchen or bathroom fixtures that seeps into adjacent wood.

Drips, mildew, water stains and soil erosion indicate excessive moisture. If you can't eliminate the condition that causes excessive moisture, try to improve the ventilation of the affected area so that air currents can help dry it out.

7) Infested tree stumps. Dead tree stumps are an excellent breeding ground for subterranean termites. Pull out any that you find in unexcavated areas underneath your home or in nearby areas outside.

8) Formboards left in place. Formboards made of plywood or lumber are often used when pouring concrete foundations, floors, sidewalks, etc. If they're left in place after construction is completed,

The heavy growth of vines in front of this outdoor staircase trapped rainwater and kept the sun from drying out the wood structure. The resulting condition of excessive moisture triggered fungi to grow and soften this support post.

Planter boxes may be attractive, but they provide wood-rotting fungi with a constant source of moisture. This box dripped water down the side of the porch where it sat and accelerated the porch's decay.

Fences are often built less carefully and decay more quickly than homes. An attached fence may conduct fungi to an otherwise sound home, so it should be inspected regularly for infestation.

they provide food for subterranean termites and often serve as a bridge between the earth and the wooden structure of the house. Remove formboards and wooden stakes. If the wood is embedded in the concrete and won't come out, cut away as much as possible and treat the rest with wood preservative.

9) Additions without proper foundations. Additions to homes, especially porches and decks, are sometimes built by people without a thorough knowledge of construction techniques. Their foundations may not meet building codes. Check foundations that appear to have been added on after your home was built. Make sure concrete footings, drainage, ventilation, and grade level are adequate. Watch out for earth-wood contact.

10) Planter boxes. If planter boxes are attached to your house, water from them can drain behind the exterior siding and cause fungus decay and termite infestation. Unattached boxes placed on wood decking or against siding can trap moisture and cause the same problems. Move the boxes, if possible, and probe for decayed wood with a screwdriver. If the boxes themselves are rotting, decay of adjacent wood surfaces won't be far behind. Remove rotting boxes and adjacent uninfected ones, since the chances of their decay are high. Repair decayed wood found behind them. If the box must be replaced, it should be redesigned with adequate flashings and drainage.

11) Fences and posts. Ideally, wood fences and posts should rest on or above concrete, bolted to a U-shaped metal anchor embedded in the concrete. If the wood must go into the ground, it should be pressure-treated with a wood preservative or else termites might infest it.

When fences are freestanding, the fence alone risks infestation. When fences are attached to the home, they can serve as a conduit for infestations to the main structure. Check wood fences for decay and termite infestation, especially at the bases of main posts that enter the ground. Check the siding of your home where fences, railings, or other abutments are attached. If you find decayed or infested wood, replace it, treat adjacent areas with chemical wood preservative and repair as necessary.

12) Abutments, columns, balusters, etc. Everything mentioned about fences also goes for abutments and other attached structures. When these structures are hollow (constructed of stucco or other siding over framed lumber) termites or decay are more difficult, but no less important, to detect. Tap the abutment in several places, listen for differences in sound, and make inspection holes where you suspect an infestation. The remedy for an infested abutment depends upon the siding material. It usually requires you to remove the surface, replace damaged wood, and rebuild the structure using techniques that discourage reinfestation.

13) Exterior doors and jambs. This inspection should include the main doors of your home (front, back, side, deck, basement, etc.) as well as access doors for gas, electrical and water meter cabinets and inspection doors for plumbing. Probe corners carefully with a screwdriver—you may find damage that would otherwise have gone undetected. Replace any damaged elements you find.

14) Porches, balconies and landings. If these structures have wood floors, they're especially susceptible to decay. If they're made of non-wood materials such as concrete or steel, they can contribute to decay at the points where they're attached to the house. These points should be examined carefully for decay.

Abutments add to a home's charm, but they may hide decay. Until this column (above) began to collapse under its own weight, no one suspected the extent of the decay beneath (see photo below).

Probe the corners of door jambs with a screwdriver. Moisture tends to collect here. You could find a hidden infestation that has begun to hollow out the entire frame.

Leaky porch floors contribute to decay in the subarea though leaks may not be visible. This pest control inspector is water-testing a concrete-covered porch with a wood subfloor that was recently repaired (above left). Underneath, water still seeps into the wood (below). If the porch had been repaired correctly, it could have passed this test and could have been assured against repeated repairs in the near future.

Substructure (basement or crawlspace)

For this stage of the tour, you'll need old clothes or overalls, gloves, an old screwdriver with a medium-sized blade and the best flashlight you can get your hands on. The basement or crawlspace, if there is one, presents you with the largest area of exposed wood in the house. A careful inspection of the substructure from this space can tell you a lot about the condition of a home.

Keep in mind the conditions that you looked for while walking around the outside of the house. You'll need to relate some of the conditions you find inside the substructure to what you observed outside. Inspect all floor joists, visible subfloor, wall studs, sheathing, mudsills, bearing beams and columns, wood doors, wood vents, etc.—everything accessible that's made of wood. Use the screwdriver to probe any suspicious surface or crevice. Move any stored boxes or furniture that prevent you from making a thorough inspection. If cobwebs or dirt hide the wood, get a hand brush or vacuum and clean the area until you can get a better look.

The accessibility of the substructure depends upon the kind of foundation your home has. Many new homes rest on concrete slab foundations that completely cover the earth under the structure. They have no crawlspace or basement at all, so you can only inspect the features of the foundation visi-

ble from the exterior grade level. Luckily, slab foundations usually keep the substructure free of infestation. Houses with basement foundations and perimeter wall foundations are usually older and more vulnerable to structural pests. Both foundations are made of continuous concrete footings along the perimeter of the house. Basement substructures are easy to walk around in, but structural elements such as the mudsill and studs may be hidden by paneling. Perimeter wall foundations provide little more than an earth-floored crawlspace under the house, but the wood structural elements are seldom hidden by finished surfaces.

Checklist 2: Substructure

1) ☐ Evidence of infestation
2) ☐ Earth-wood contacts
3) ☐ Faulty grade
4) ☐ Shower leaks
5) ☐ Plumbing leaks
6) ☐ Condensation from improperly vented appliances
7) ☐ Ventilation
8) ☐ Excessive moisture
9) ☐ Infested tree stumps
10) ☐ Formboards left in place
11) ☐ Additions without proper foundations
12) ☐ Cellulose debris

This piece of a floor joist is riddled with subterranean termite galleries and is no longer capable of supporting a house's weight.

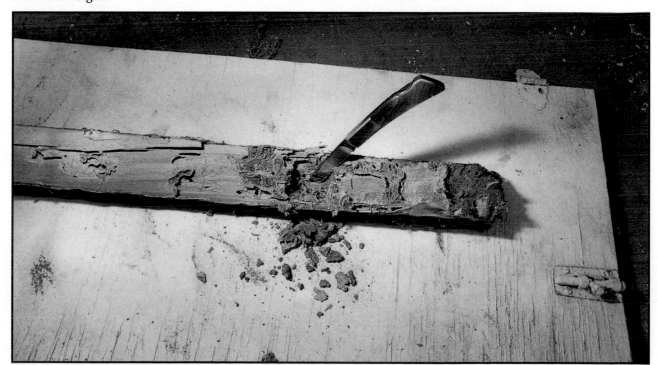

1) Evidence of infestation. Look for subterranean termites (shelter tubes, damaged wood), dampwood termites (moisture, damaged wood), drywood termites (pellets, damaged wood, wings from swarmers), beetles (wood riddled with tiny holes which are powdery when tapped) and fungi (moisture, water stains, discolored wood, white thread-like growth).

2) Earth-wood contacts. Contact between earth and the wood substructure is as much a hazard inside the home as it is outside. Ground moisture can lead to fungus damage even if rain water never touches the wood directly, and it makes termite infestation much more likely to occur. As a rule of thumb, there should be a six-inch clearance between the ground under the house and all substructural members. Eliminate earth-wood contacts here, as you should outside, by removing excess dirt or by capping the foundation.

Watch out for wood that is embedded in concrete (redwood mudsills, though, are o.k.) and re-move it, if possible. If you can't, treat it with a wood preservative.

3) Faulty grade. If you weren't able to judge the adequacy of the grade level outside because you couldn't see the mudsills there, finish that examination from here. You may need to do some estimating to relate the exterior grade to the height of interior mudsills. Compare the vertical distance of each from benchmarks such as the lower edge of a window or the location where a watermain pipe enters the house. In some places, it may be useful to drill a small pilot hole through the siding at the upper edge of the mudsill as a benchmark. Later, this hole should be caulked or filled with a plug. In addition, check the grade level wherever concrete piers support wood foundation posts.

If you find places where the bottom of the mudsill is even with the exterior grade, you should have the grade level lowered by raising the foundation or removing dirt. If you do the latter, be careful not to undermine the existing foundation or cause a

Substructures are often ill-kept and prone to infestation. Underneath your home you may find many different infestations and problem conditions. Subterranean termite tubes often climb along wood posts and mudsills when these structural members rest directly on the earth (1). Earth piled high near joists and mudsills (2) and scraps of wood lying directly on the earth (3) further encourage infestations. You may notice fungi or water stains on the subfloor under a toilet with a leaky lead bend (4). The mudsill may be at or below the level of the ground outside (5), which increases the chances that ground water will seep into wood substructural members, such as sheathing (6). You may also have a garden along the side of your home with a high ground level (7).

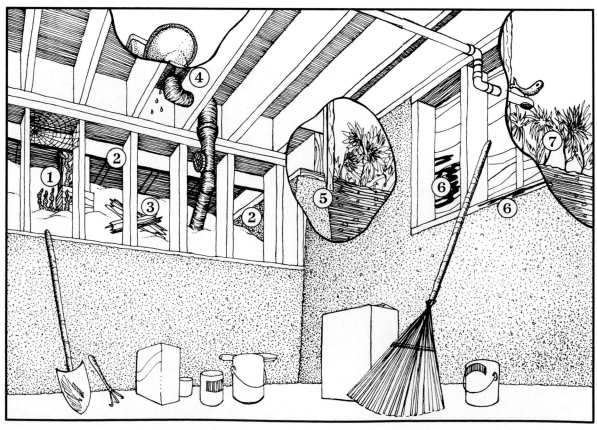

drainage problem.

You may want to consider raising the foundation or removing dirt even if your mudsill is already above the exterior grade. To help protect the substructure against infestation, the mudsill should be at least six inches above the exterior grade.

4) Shower leaks. A leaky shower stall or bathtub can rot the wood substructure beneath it. If yours leaks, you may see water stains or evidence of fungus decay there. Use a screwdriver to probe the floor joist and subfloor for decay. Water-test the shower or tub by stopping up the drain with a plug or a piece of plastic wrap. Fill the shower pan with water until it's almost overflowing. Fill the tub until water leaks out the overflow. Let the water stand for 20 minutes. Look below the shower or tub for leaks. If you find any, the shower pan or tub will have to be replaced. Decayed wood under the floor should be replaced, preferably with pressure-treated wood. The adjacent areas should be treated with a wood preservative.

5) Plumbing leaks. When leaks and condensation on plumbing pipes raise the moisture content of nearby wood over 20 percent (the wet-to-the-touch mark) for a sustained period of time, the wood will eventually decay. Look around and below all plumbing pipes for water stains or decay. Probe suspicious wood. Repair any leaks. Reduce condensation buildup by improving ventilation. Add foundation vents if necessary. If you can't prevent condensation that way, cover wood areas adjacent to or below the problem pipes with aluminum flashing that is bent so it drains water away from the wood. This is a stop-gap measure, but it will prevent moisture from building up in the wood.

6) Condensation from improperly vented appliances. When clothes dryers or other appliances that produce heat and moisture are improperly installed, the humidity may enter the substructure area instead of escaping outside through vents. Check to see that such appliances are properly vented.

If your substructure has as many problems as described on the preceeding page, you need not despair. You can solve many of them on your own if you're willing to spend a little time and energy. Break termites' shelter tubes and put concrete footings under wood posts (1). Dig earth out of the substructure until it's at least six inches lower than joists and sills (2). Remove wood and paper debris from the earth (3). Replace a leaky lead bend with a new ABS bend and rebolt the toilet (4) (Chapter 10 shows you how). If you need to correct the foundation grade level but can't lower the ground outside, you have two options (Chapter 10 gives details on both). If possible, you should cap your foundation by removing decayed siding, raising the mudsill with bolts and pouring concrete over the existing foundation (5). If the mudsill is too close to the joists to raise, you should pour a concrete curb between the siding and the exterior grade (6).

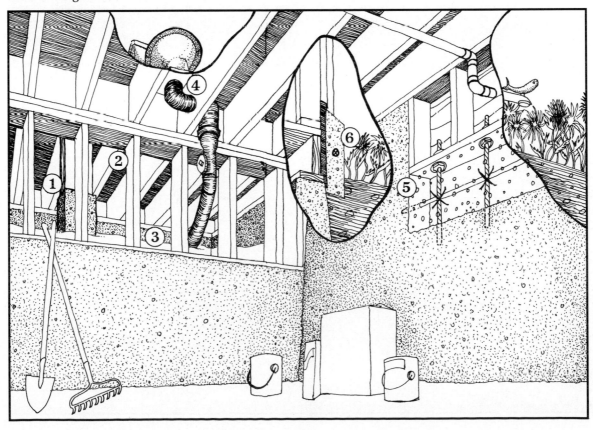

Using the lower edge of the window for reference, notice that the foundation underneath this stucco house is several inches beneath the exterior grade (top). Because of this condition, water seeps down into the substructure. Fungus has damaged the mudsill and some of the sheathing (bottom).

Furnace and hot water heater flues in the substructure can release hot gas if they are corroded or improperly installed. As heat rises, so does humidity. Check the condition of these flues and of wood nearby. You might notice condensation on leaking flues.

7) Ventilation. Even if leaks and condensation from bathrooms, plumbing pipes or appliances aren't a problem, other sources of moisture can raise the humidity level in the substructure unless this area has adequate ventilation, usually provided by vents. The building services department of your local government can probably give you a "ventilation ratio" for your basement—square inches of vent surface per hundred square feet of basement area. If ventilation under your house seems inadequate, it can't hurt to install additional vents. Make sure that the existing vents aren't clogged by vegetation or blocked by stacks of wood.

8) Excessive moisture. While all the preceding conditions contribute to excessive moisture in the substructure, the most significant causes are underground springs, high water tables and improperly drained surface water. Surface water enters the substructure through cracks in the foundation or seeps underneath it. These drainage problems are especially obvious during rainy weather. Look for water stains on concrete and wood, evidence of soil erosion and foundations that have settled.

Moisture from high water tables and underground springs can often be controlled by digging a sump hole in the lowest part of the basement and installing a water pump. A float switch turns the pump on when the water reaches a certain level in the hole. If surface water seeps into the substructure, reroute drainage of your home site as described in the first stage of the tour.

9) Infested tree stumps. The subterranean remains of trees, vines or other woody vegetation can harbor termites. If you find stumps or roots in any excavated areas, remove them if possible. If you can't, treat the area with wood preservative.

10) Formboards left in place. Remove formboards and stakes or treat them with a wood preservative.

11) Additions without proper foundations. You've already checked additions from the outside (condition 9 on the first check list)—now finish inspecting them for problems from beneath.

12) Cellulose debris. Small pieces of wood or other material made of cellulose that lie on the soil under your house serve as snacks that attract termites to the area. Once termites find debris, they move on to a larger feast—the substructure! Rake or pick up any wood-like debris in unexcavated areas, and make sure you don't store any lumber, doors, furniture, cartons, etc. directly on the soil.

Mycelia cover the wood subfloor under a leaky shower. The subfloor and joists should be replaced.

Living areas and attached structures

This middle stage of the tour will sharpen your awareness of conditions that surround you every day.

Checklist 3: Living area

1) ☐ Evidence of infestation
2) ☐ Shower leaks
3) ☐ Plumbing leaks
4) ☐ Ventilation
5) ☐ Poorly maintained floor surfaces

1) Evidence of infestation. Look for blemishes and discolorations on finished surfaces. These often indicate the presence of infestation and decay below the surface. Check wood floors (remove furniture and rugs if possible), wood door and window frames, ceilings and beams, paneling and built-in cabinets. If you see something suspicious, probe carefully with a screwdriver or the point of a knife.

Move any appliances that aren't built-in and inspect behind and beneath them. Take off the front panel of built-in dishwashers, wall heaters, water heater closets, etc. to look for signs of infestation— but remember to turn off the power first.

2) Shower leaks. You've already looked for leaks in the shower pan or bathtub from below. Sometimes, you can also see them from inside the bathroom, along with leaks and defects in the stall's walls. Check the pan and walls for water stains, cracks, loose grout, a loose soap dish or other loose fittings (including the flanges that form a trim around the shower head pipe and hot and cold water valves). Use your nose, too. Sniff around for a musty, mildewy odor that persists even after the bathroom has just been cleaned. It may indicate that water is seeping behind the tile or other waterproof surface that lines the shower enclosure.

Leaking plumbing fixtures and loose tiles aren't just cosmetic problems. They allow moisture into the substructure and accelerate the decay of your home. In your bathroom, check for: leaks at the base of the toilet (1), which mean you'll need to rebolt the toilet (see Chapter 10 for instructions); leaks in the shower threshold that allow water to splash onto the floor (2); leaks in the shower pan (3), which mean you'll need a new one (see Chapter 10); gaps between tub and floor, which—if the subfloor beneath isn't already rotted out—should be caulked and sealed (4); and leaks in faucets, shower heads and water valves that allow water to seep behind loose tile (5).

The loose tiles around this tub allow water to seep into the walls and floor, where fungi may be flourishing. The only way to assess the extent of the damage and to make repairs is to remove tiling.

Water from the shower seeped under the floor of this bathroom until the wood subfloor outside the shower stall rotted all the way through (above right and below). The floor covering and stall tiling have been removed so the stall and the subfloor can be replaced.

If you find evidence of leaks, you may need to remove tiles or wall boards to confirm the source. Repair leaks and replace defective materials. Replace damaged wood members. Caulk loose plumbing trim.

3) Plumbing leaks. Check for leaks under the kitchen and bathroom sinks (remove plumbing inspection plates to do this if there are any), around the sink cabinet and toilet. Repair any leaks and replace damaged wood.

4) Ventilation. Inadequate ventilation causes moisture to collect on cold surfaces. Wood frame windows are highly susceptible to decay from condensed moisture because glass panes are often much colder than the air inside. Check all such windows by probing the corners near the glass, especially the lower ones, with a small screwdriver. Decayed windows need to be repaired or replaced —a costly procedure.

The kitchen and bathroom tend to be especially vulnerable to ventilation problems. Hot water used while cooking or bathing produces excessive humidity in enclosed areas, and this encourages decay.

5) Poorly maintained floor surfaces. Cracked tiles and linoleum, worn vinyl flooring or loose grout in kitchen and bathroom floors allow water to seep between the flooring and the subfloor. A small amount of water here may do a lot of damage because the flooring prevents the wood beneath it from drying out. Check kitchen and bathroom floors for these flaws. Caulk flooring along the edges of bathtubs, shower pans or toilet bases so cracks there are well sealed. Tile floors contain many other seams that you should check. If you find cracks in areas where water often falls, you may want to lift a tile to inspect the subfloor—a major repair job may be necessary.

Attic area

An inspection of the attic can tell you quite a bit about the condition of the roof. You may discover leaks, for example, that have caused decay in the upper structure of your home.

Getting into the attic is the first obstacle in this stage of the tour. If your house doesn't have a staircase or built-in ladder leading to the attic, look for an access hole in a hallway or closet ceiling that you can open by using a step ladder. If you can't find any access to the attic or if the existing one is too difficult to use, it may be worthwhile to have an access hole installed in a convenient place. This will make regular attic inspections easier.

The second obstacle is the attic's vertical clearance. If your home has a shallow roof pitch, the height of the attic at its peak may leave barely enough room for crawling. If you can't move around up there carefully, you run the risk of cracking the ceiling plaster or sheetrock in the room below. In these cases, you can sometimes see enough of the attic to make the inspection by standing on a step ladder with your body extending through the access hole. In any case, you'll need to take a powerful flashlight with you.

Insulation poses the third obstacle. It helps keep the temperature in your house comfortable throughout the seasons, but it makes inspecting ceiling joists much more difficult. If the insulation is made of fiberglass, wear gloves, a dust mask, a long-sleeved shirt and pants. (Fiberglass may be as dangerous as asbestos. Wash these clothes separately from the rest of your laundry or you may find yourself with a case of itchiness for a few weeks.) If you notice any suspicious areas in the wood, you may need to remove the insulation to get a better look.

Checklist 4: Attic

1) ☐ Evidence of infestation
2) ☐ Roof system
3) ☐ Ventilation

1) Evidence of infestation. Look for wings, pellets, and sealed entry holes left by drywood termites. Sometimes, even subterranean termites, dampwood termites, and beetles make their way to the attic.

Plumbing leaks damage wood in the kitchen as well as the bathroom. Leaky fixtures spill water over the kitchen counter (1, left). Water seeps behind loose tile (2, left) or under the sink tub (3, left). Look under the sink cabinet. If wood is stained by water or discolored by fungi (4, below), you should have the wood replaced as well as the fixtures.

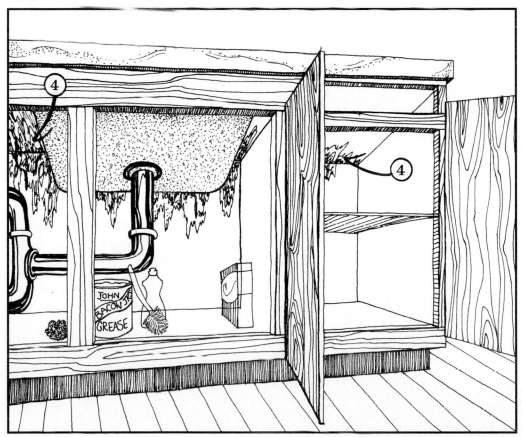

2) Roof system. Inspect the underside of the roof—wood or plywood sheathing as well as rafters—for water stains and fungus growth. Carefully check areas where plumbing pipes, vents, fireplace and heating flues penetrate the roof line. This is where the roof is most likely to fail.

3) Ventilation. If the roof leaks or if water blows into the attic during very windy storms, good ventilation allows wood to dry out before fungus decay sets in. During summer months, in addition, ventilation reduces the heat that builds up in the attic and keeps the temperature in the rest of the house more comfortable.

Roof and exterior walls

This tour concludes with a climb to the roof and higher reaches of the outside walls. Take a ladder with you as you walk around the house once again and check eaves, upper parts of windows and doors, and attached structures such as decks, balconies, and landings. Climbing a ladder, especially to get onto the roof, always involves some risk. Use a ladder appropriate to the height you have to climb and the terrain below. If you need advice about ladders, consult a rental supply or hardware store. Don't attempt to climb if you doubt your ability to do it safely.

Discoloration at the corner of a stucco house usually means that water has seeped behind the siding from the gutter. Decay here is well underway.

Checklist 5: Roof and exterior walls

1) ☐ Evidence of infestation
2) ☐ Cracks in exterior walls
3) ☐ Porches, decks, balconies, and landings
4) ☐ Roof system

1) Evidence of infestation. Once again, look for discolorations or blemishes that might indicate infestation or defects in your home's exterior water seal. Use a screwdriver to probe suspicious areas in wood, stucco, and other materials.

2) Cracks in exterior walls. Rain water that penetrates cracks in exterior walls can cause extensive damage to wood sheathing, especially if moisture is trapped beneath an air-tight surface (such as stucco, oil-base paint, or aluminum or asbestos siding). Unfinished wood siding made of cedar or redwood shingles (which contain natural preservatives) has an advantage over air-tight surfaces because it allows water to escape as vapor and reduces the risk of fungus damage.

Cracks are often found at the corners of windows and doors, along chimneys and at points where decks, porches, steps, fences and other abutments attach to the house. If your home has several different roof levels, check for cracks along the lines where lower roofs attach to the side of the house.

Probe any cracks or breaks in the siding surface to see how much of the wood structure underneath has decayed, if at all. If the siding is wood, you may be able to probe the sheathing without removing any siding. If you do find damage there, though, the siding will eventually have to be removed. If the siding is stucco, a small section—about two inches in diameter—must be removed in order to probe wood sheathing for decay.

3) Porches, decks, balconies, and landings. Check these structures and the points at which they're attached to the house. If the structure is wood, decay is most likely to occur wherever water can be trapped. For example, the structure may contain boards that intersect or lie close together in such a way that they trap water or moisture-retaining debris. Depressions in wood left by nail heads or hammer blows and areas beneath furniture and plants are likely spots for decay. If possible, check the undersides of porches, decks, etc. for evidence of decay and infestation. If the structure extends to the ground, you should already have checked it for faulty grade, earth-wood contact, excessive moisture, formboards and wood embedded in concrete.

The gutter that you see at the center of this picture is designed to collect water that runs off the roof and around the shingles. However, many such gutters leak and allow water to seep into the wood behind the stucco siding, where it is trapped. In addition, flat roofs don't direct water to the gutters efficiently and puddles tend to linger on the roof after a heavy rain.

Although this roof doesn't have gutters, the slope of the roof and its generous overhang do a much better job of directing rainwater away from the side of the house than most gutters do. The ends of the roof rafters are sealed with paint against rainwater and the roof is well-maintained. These help to preserve the upper frame and windows of this house.

If the structure is stucco or other non-wood material, it's usually more difficult to evaluate. Look for cracks, water stains, and discolorations. Evaluate the condition of wood sheathing by probing with a screwdriver or by making inspection holes. If you find decay or infestation, remove the stucco covering and replace the wood.

4) Roof system. Approach your roof cautiously—you risk falling off and hurting yourself, as well as damaging a weak roof and making it leak before its time. Nonetheless, an inspection of roof and gutters can reveal much about the condition of a home.

First, evaluate the overall condition of the roof.
a) Composition shingles: Do shingles look fresh? Do they have well-defined, straight edges with plenty of mineral particles embedded in them? Do they show much weathering and expose the felt material underneath? Are any shingles torn, missing, or bent by the wind?
b) Tar and gravel: Does gravel cover the roof uniformly, or are there large, exposed patches or black tar? Is exposed tar smooth and shiny or cracked and dull? Are there large bubbles in the tar (especially during warm weather)? If so, avoid walking on these bubbles.
c) Wood shingles or shakes: Probe wood for evidence of fungus decay and termite or beetle infestation. Are any shingles split or warped?

Wood landings and stairs—especially those attached to stucco houses (above)—are often the sites of fungus infestation. Rainwater is trapped between the boards (below) and conducted toward the stucco siding.

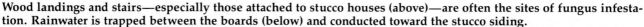

Moisture accumulates in the substructure next to the landing and stairs. You can see how fungi trace the position of the stairs under this house (above). From there, water runs down the studs so that the bases of many of them, like this one, are rotted out (below).

Do moss or leaves block water channels between the shingles? Does the shade of overhanging trees keep any roof areas damp?

Next, inspect the flashing at the chimney, plumbing vents, heater flues, electrical service (don't touch!) and anything else that goes through the roof. Look for rusted flashing material, cracked tar or other conditions that might let water leak through. If you noticed water stains during the attic inspection, check the spot above them on the roof for suspicious conditions.

Finally, examine gutters and leaders for rust (if galvanized steel), decay (if wood) and blockage. Examine eaves for decay, especially near gutters. Repair roof defects (such as cracks) and replace decayed wood.

Chapter 6

The Pest Control Report

By now, you should understand how pests infest a home and what resources you can call on to combat them. Now it's time to examine the most important document in the world of pest control—the report—prepared by the operator after an inspection.

Taking the plunge

Regulations about the content and accuracy of structural pest reports vary dramatically from state to state. Some, like California, specify, in detail, how operators should report the findings of pest control inspections, while some states don't even provide general guidelines. Additionally, California requires operators to file reports with the Structural Pest Control Board. Anyone can obtain a copy of any report filed with the board in the last two years by paying a two-dollar fee. In some other states the report, if prepared at all, is an informal document with no special legal significance.

Because so many aspects of the pest control process depend on the language of the report, it is essential to learn how to read one. It's also important to judge how adequately the report was prepared. The report should be reviewed in the same way as a legal contract. If the report is hastily compiled, sloppily or vaguely written, the consumer has little protection under the law because the terms of the report are unclear.

Occasionally, an inspector may have confidence that the operator's work crew can repair all evident infestation and decay, as well as some spots that were inaccessible to the inspector, without detailed instruction. The inspector may not consider it necessary to report findings in complete detail. A poorly prepared report can thus conceal a competent inspection as well as a superficial one. Regardless of what an inspector's motives are for writing a vague report, homeowners should have little faith in such a report. If a dispute with the operator should arise later, a vague document might not be an adequate guarantee of the operator's work.

Unfortunately, few industry-wide standards exist for inspecting homes or for documenting findings. The notation system used by inspectors can't tell you precisely how much of a substructure is infested with termites or how much of a foundation should be capped.

To show you how the inspection report works, the author has drawn up a house that has structural characteristics typical of many American homes. It's plagued with the structural pest infestations and conditions that operators encounter most frequently. These problems are reported here in a "Standard Structural Pest Control Inspection Report" from California. You may never receive a report that lists as many problems. You may, however, recognize a few of them from your own experiences with structural pests.

Following the report is a key to the codes, diagrams, and shorthand notation that operators use to report their findings. In addition to the report, operators present their clients with a contract and work authorization form. This chapter ends with California's "Standard Notice of Work Completed and Not Completed," which accounts for the condition of the house after operators have completed their work.

This house contains structural details typical of American homes. Like the real homes on which this model's based, there are defects that call for the attention of a structural pest control operator. The wood steps, in direct contact with the earth, have begun to decay (1). The garage door casing may soon begin to decay because it's embedded in concrete (2). The planter box (3) and bannister (4) hide decayed wood under stucco surfaces. The substructural support under the threshold of the front door is also decayed (5). The foundation isn't high enough above the exterior grade (6). The fungus-infested stucco arch has begun to break away from the house (7). The window sash is rotted (8). Gutters leak (9). The deck's water-proof covering has also leaked and fungi have weakened the framing (10). Other problems underneath and inside of the house are revealed in the structural pest control inspection report.

STANDARD STRUCTURAL PEST CONTROL INSPECTION REPORT
(WOOD-DESTROYING PESTS OR ORGANISMS)
This is an inspection report only - not a Notice of Completion.

ADDRESS OF PROPERTY INSPECTED	BLDG. NO. 2001	STREET Maple Street	CITY Anytown CO. CODE 01	DATE OF INSPECTION 6-14-88

FIRM NAME AND ADDRESS
A-TERMITE Control
125 Main Street
Anytown, USA 00000-0000 (003) 555-7000

Affix stamp here on Board copy only

↓ **A LICENSED PEST CONTROL** ↓
OPERATOR IS AN EXPERT IN HIS FIELD. ANY QUESTIONS RELATIVE TO THIS REPORT SHOULD BE REFERRED TO HIM.

FIRM LICENSE NO. 1234	CO. REPORT NO. (if any)	STAMP NO. 127986A

Inspection Ordered by (Name and Address) Sherry Nordstrom, Sure-Sale Realty 4000 Pleasant Dr., Anytown

Report Sent to (Name and Address) Sherry Nordstrom, Sure-Sale Realty 4000 Pleasant Dr., Anytown, USA

Owner's Name and Address Leah Cordova, 2001 Maple St., Anytown, USA

Name and Address of a Party in Interest Reliable Mortgage, 123 River St., Anytown, USA

Original Report [XX] Supplemental Report [ ] Limited Report [ ] Reinspection Report [ ] No. of Pages: 4

YES	CODE	SEE DIAGRAM BELOW	YES	CODE	SEE DIAGRAM BELOW	YES	CODE	SEE DIAGRAM BELOW	YES	CODE	SEE DIAGRAM BELOW
X	S-Subterranean Termites		X	B-Beetles-Other Wood Pests			Z-Dampwood Termites		X	EM-Excessive Moisture Condition	
X	K-Dry-Wood Termites		X	FG-Faulty Grade Levels		X	SL-Shower Leaks		X	IA-Inaccessible Areas	
X	F-Fungus or Dry Rot		X	EC-Earth-wood Contacts		X	CD-Cellulose Debris		X	FI-Further Inspection Recom.	

1. SUBSTRUCTURE AREA (soil conditions, accessibility, etc.) Dry, partially inaccessible.
2. Was Stall Shower water tested? Yes. Did floor coverings indicate leaks? Yes.
3. FOUNDATIONS (Type, Relation to Grade, etc.) Concrete, below grade.
4. PORCHES ... STEPS ... PATIOS Wood frame. No patio.
5. VENTILATION (Amount, Relation to Grade, etc.) Inadequate.
6. ABUTMENTS ... Stucco walls, columns, arches, etc. Stucco exterior.
7. ATTIC SPACES (accessibility, insulation, etc.) Accessible.
8. GARAGES (Type, accessibility, etc.) Attached, accessible.
9. OTHER Other observations noted in section 9 below.

DIAGRAM AND EXPLANATION OF FINDINGS (This report is limited to structure or structures shown on diagram.)

General Description Wood frame, stucco side-wall/wood siding exterior, attached garage, occupied single family dwelling. Inspection Tag Posted (location) Subarea framing.

Other Inspection Tags None noted.

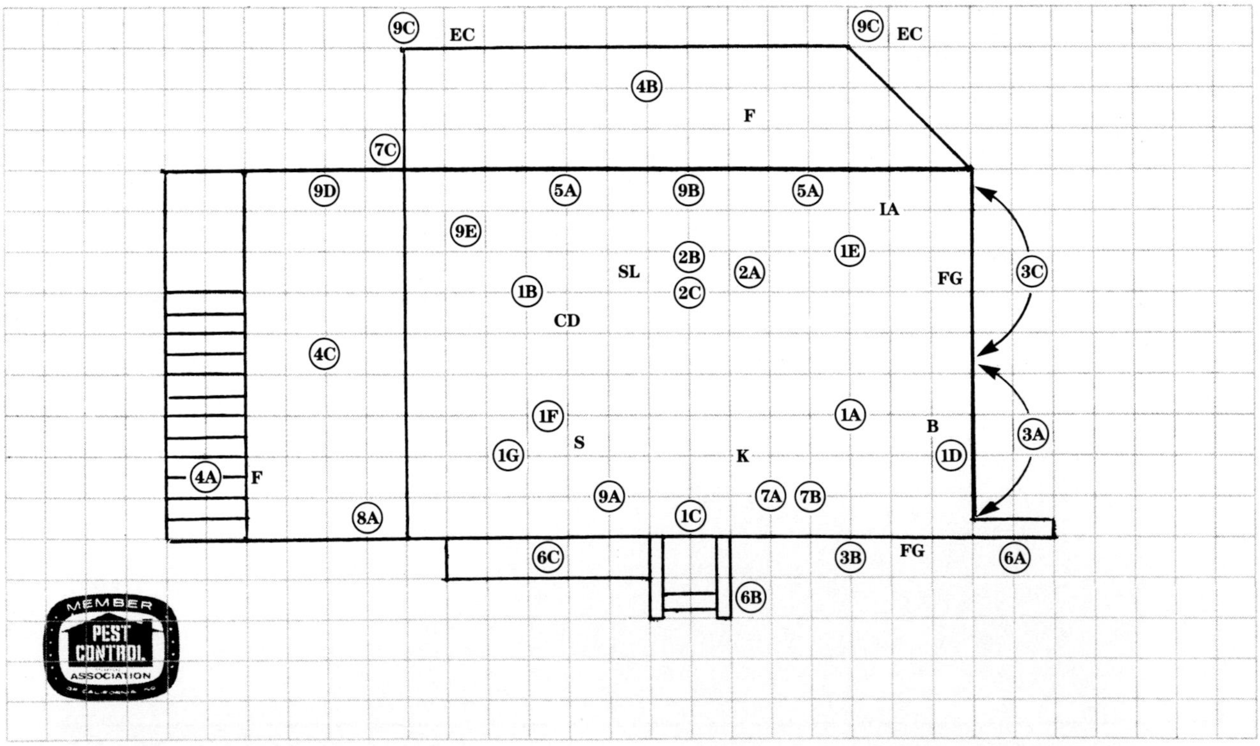

Inspected by Michael Smith License No. AA 1234 Signature _Michael Smith_

Page 2 of standard inspection report of the property located at:
2001 Maple Street, Anytown
Stamp number: 127986A **Date of inspection:** 6-14-88

SUBSTRUCTURE AREA

1A Finding: (Information only) Articles are stored on the subarea floor. Wood storage shelves are in direct contact with earth.

Recommendation: Remove the stored articles and shelves. This report does not include removal of stored articles and shelves by A-TERMITE Control.

Note: A-TERMITE Control will not issue a structural pest control certification until this item has been completed.

1B Finding: Cellulose debris was noted on the subarea soil.

Recommendation: Rake all soil surface in the subarea and haul away the accumulated debris.

1C Finding: The support framing underneath the door threshold is fungus deteriorated.

Recommendation: Cut out all fungus-deteriorated wood members and repair with new wood. Repair the threshold and flooring surfaces to match existing finish as closely as possible.

1D Finding: Wood-boring beetle emergence holes and damage are evident in the access door. The damage appears to be limited to the access door.

Recommendation: Remove the access door and install a new door to match as closely as possible. No chemical treatment is required because the damage appears to be confined to the access door.

Note: The owner is to schedule frequent inspections of this area to better monitor this situation.

1E Finding: This area of the substructure is inaccessible for normal inspection due to piled soil against the floor joists. This also constitutes earth-wood contact.

Recommendation: Excavate the soil to leave a 12-inch clearance under the joists and eliminate earth-wood contacts. Repair any damaged wood members with new wood.

1F Finding: Subterranean termite tubes were observed near a pier rise.

Recommendation: Scrape down all subterranean termite shelter tubes in the visible, accessible areas.

1G Finding: The source of the subterranean termite infestation described in this report is a colony in the ground.

Recommendation: Control the subterranean termite infestation by properly applying a termiticide chemical barrier in the soil of the local area.

STALL SHOWER

2A Finding: (Information only) Master bathroom shower was water-tested. No leakage was noted at the time of this inspection.

Recommendation: The owner is to schedule periodic inspections of the shower. This report does not include any repairs, such as sealing of the shower, by A-TERMITE Control.

TUB WALL COVERINGS

2B Finding: The tub and shower stall walls leak. Fungus deterioration in the subfloor beneath tub extends under the surrounding floor area.

Recommendation: Remove the wall coverings around the tub. Remove all fungus-deteriorated wood members and repair with new wood. Install a new subfloor and standard grade vinyl floor covering, neutral color. Install new waterproof sheetrock and a new standard grade ceramic tile wall covering around the tub and shower enclosures, neutral color.

COMMODE

See item 2C.

FLOOR COVERINGS

2C Finding: Damaged floor covering around the toilet in rear of bathroom.

Recommendation: Remove the toilet. Remove all damaged floor covering and deteriorated wood members. Treat the area with a fungicide if necessary and repair with new wood. Install a standard grade vinyl floor covering, neutral color. Install a new wax seal at the base of the toilet and rebolt the toilet.

Page 3 of standard inspection report of the property located at:
2001 Maple Street, Anytown
Stamp number: 127986A **Date of inspection:** 6-14-88

FOUNDATION

3A   Finding: Fungus deterioration noted in the lower framing and sill.
Recommendation: Increase the height of the foundation by installing a steel-reinforced concrete cap and a new sill.
3B   Finding: The top of the foundation wall is below grade level.
Recommendation: Properly grade the exterior soil to eliminate the faulty grade condition.
3C   Finding: The foundation is below the exterior grade level. It is not practical to grade the soil or increase the height of the foundation. No fungus deterioration is evident at this time.
Recommendation: Install a metal-flashed, steel-reinforced concrete curb wall along the exterior to protect the wood members below grade.

PORCHES/STEPS

4A   Finding: The wood-constructed steps, landing (side), carriage and stringer[1] exhibit fungus deterioration.
Recommendation: Remove all of the steps and landing and rebuild with new wood to comply with current building codes. Prime paint only.
4B   Finding: The wood-constructed rear deck wood framing and decking exhibit fungus deterioration.
Recommendation: Remove fungus-deteriorated wood members and repair with new wood. Prime paint new wood only.
4C   Finding: The upper side deck waterproof covering has failed. The supporting wood framing and plywood soffit[2] exhibit fungus deterioration.
Recommendation: Remove the existing waterproof covering. Cut out all fungus-deteriorated wood members and repair with new wood, prime paint exposed wood members only. Install a new gray waterproof covering (Chemtex).

PATIO

None

VENTILATION

5A   Finding: Subarea ventilation is inadequate.
Recommendation: Install 4" x 6" vents as necessary.

ABUTMENTS

6A   Finding: The stucco arch is pulling away from the dwelling and the supporting wood members exhibit fungus deterioration.
Recommendation: Remove stucco arch and and all fungus-deteriorated wood members. Repair with new wood and restucco corner to match existing finish as closely as possible. Prime paint disturbed areas only.
6B   Finding: The front stucco bannister framing exhibits fungus deterioration.
Recommendation: Remove the exterior stucco and all fungus-deteriorated wood members. Repair with new wood and treat the wood with a fungicide if necessary. Restucco to match the existing finish as closely as possible. Prime paint disturbed areas only.
6C   Finding: The front stucco planter framing exhibits fungus deterioration.
Recommendation: Break open the top of planter sides and strip out the wood framing. Fill the resulting voids with concrete. Restucco top to match existing finish as closely as possible. Prime paint disturbed areas only.

ATTIC SPACE

7A   Finding: A small drywood termite infestation was observed in the wood support framing. No significant structural damage was observed. The wood members do not appear to have lost their ability to properly support the dwelling.

---

[1] The carriage and stringers are the diagonal beams and upright posts that support a flight of stairs from beneath.

[2] The soffit, as used here, is the underpart of deck. The underparts of stairways, eaves, arches and other features are also soffits.

Page 4 of standard inspection report of the property located at:
2001 Maple Street, Anytown
Stamp number: 127986A **Date of inspection:** 6-14-88

Recommendation: Cover the holes with masking tape and recheck for signs of new termite activity to determine whether this is a prior or recent infestation. The wood members are to remain in their present condition. Further inspection of this area is required.

7B Finding: Drywood termite pellets were observed in the attic space.

Recommendation: Remove all drywood termite pellets in the visible, accessible areas, so that this situation can be easily monitored in the future.

Note: This item is to be completed in conjunction with item **7A**. After further inspection has been completed, recommendations for drywood termite control will be outlined in a supplemental report.

7C Finding: The corner exhibits moisture penetration from the gutters.

Recommendation: Further inspection. This area is to be opened and inspected. Findings will be outlined in a supplemental report. The cost of the further inspection will be provided upon request. This report does not include inspection nor possible repairs in this area by A-TERMITE Control.

GARAGE

8A Finding: The base of the door casings are embedded in concrete.

Recommendation: Cut off the base of the door casings and fill the resulting voids with concrete.

OTHER OBSERVATIONS

9A Finding: There is evidence of moisture penetration and fungus deterioration along the gutter line.

Recommendation: Remove all damaged wood members and repair with new wood. Prime paint new wood only.

Note: The owner is to consult with a person specializing in this area for inspection of the roof, gutter and downspout system of the entire structure, and to make all necessary repairs to prevent further damage, after pest control repairs have been completed.

9B Finding: One wood six-lite[3] outswinging casement window sash is fungus deteriorated.

Recommendation: Replace the wood window with one of like design and quality. Prime paint only.

9C Finding: The supporting wood posts are in direct contact with earth.

Recommendation: Cut off the base of the wood posts and install concrete piers.

9D Finding: The rear basement door exhibits fungus deterioration.

Recommendation: Replace the basement door. Prime paint only. Reuse existing hardware.

9E Finding: The supporting wood members under the kitchen counter top exhibit fungus deterioration.

Recommendation: Remove the counter top and sink. Repair all damaged wood members with new wood. Install a new counter top and reset the sink.

DISCLAIMER

All recommendations in our report should be completed. A-TERMITE Control assumes no responsibility for infestations or infections that may result if recommendations are not completed by this company.

If work is performed by others, we cannot certify that this structure is free of infestations or infections unless this company is contacted to reinspect the structure prior to closing of any areas. An additional charge will be required for reinspection of all work performed by others.

A-TERMITE Control guarantees the work completed by this company for a period of one year from the date of completion with the exception of plumbing, grouting, and resetting of commodes, tubs and shower stalls, which are guaranteed for thirty (30) days only.

All work is subject to the approval of the local building department. If the building department requires additional work, this will be contracted separately.

See the attached Work Authorization for the cost of recommended items. An authorized signature is necessary before work can be performed.

---

[3] A lite is a pane of glass in a window, separated from other lites by wood moulding. A solid-pane window has one lite. A window divided into four parts by vertical and horizontal mouldings has 4 lites. The more lites a window has, the more expensive it is to replace.

Key to Standard Structural Pest Control Inspection Report

Part I: Identification

The first section of the report identifies the property and persons involved in the inspection. It's important that the information on each line is correct.

1) **Address of property inspected.** Property may be a house, apartment, garage, store, etc.

2) **County code.**

3) **Date of inspection.** Pest control operators in California must mail a copy of the report to interested parties within five days of this date.

4) **Firm name and address.** This is the legal or dba name of the pest control operator and the address of the local office from which the operator works.

5) **Firm license number.** This is given by those states that license pest control operators.

6) **Company report number.** This is the operator's internal reference number.

7) **Stamp number.** In California, a stamp issued by the Structural Pest Control Board must be attached to each report filed with the state. Proceeds from the sale of these stamps support the board's activities, including investigation of consumer complaints.

8) **Name and address of person who ordered report.** Usually, the party with the greatest financial interest in the property orders the report—the homeowner, buyer or seller. Occasionally, real estate agents or contractors order the report in their name on behalf of the buyer or seller.

9) **Name and address of person to whom report is sent.** The report is usually sent to the owner. If a real estate transaction depends upon the report, copies may be sent to an agent who will distribute them to interested parties.

10) **Owner's name and address.**

11) **Name and address of a party in interest.** The names of the seller, buyer, buyer's mortgage lender and all agents should be listed here, unless listed above. Make sure that all interested parties are named on lines 9 through 11.

12) **Original report, supplemental report, limited report or reinspection report.** The inspector checks the box that describes the report. An original report is not necessarily the first report on the property, but the first by the inspector's company. A supplemental report adds to the information contained in the original.* A reinspection report accounts for the condition of all previously inspected areas after another contractor has completed repairs. In this case, the report serves as the certification of the home's condition and as the notice of completion.* A limited report describes the condition of only a part of the building. Buyers should regard limited reports with suspicion, since they may omit areas that are extensively damaged.

13) **Number of pages.** Make sure you receive the number of pages indicated. Sometimes the last page of the report, which may contain the bad news, never makes its way into the hands of the buyer.

14) **Name of licensed inspector of the property.**

15) **State license number of inspector above.**

Part II: Findings

You're already familiar with the kinds of problems that inspectors check for. The chart of 12 letter codes at the beginning of this section lists most of the types of problems or infestations that could be discovered by an inspector (some you may have noticed while inspecting your own home). A mark in the box to the left of any code (such as "K - Drywood termites" or "CD -Cellulose debris") indicates that the inspector found that infestation or problem condition. Notice that the model home is beset with just about every problem in the book.

A check next to the "Inaccessible Area" code means that an area in the home, accessible in most other homes, cannot be inspected because of some physical barrier. If the inspector suspects that this area might conceal structural damage, the "Further Inspection Recommended" box is marked. If your own knowledge of the house leads you to believe that an inaccessible area conceals damage, remove the barriers before the inspection. This may be as simple as removing storage boxes or it may require removing paneling, but it can save you the expense of further inspection.

A second chart enumerates nine areas of a property that are subject to infestation. Brief notes describe the condition or construction of each area.

---

* For examples of a supplemental report and a reinspection report, see Appendix 3.

If any one of these areas is not inspected because it is inaccessible, the inspector indicates that here. For example, attic space is often described as inaccessible because it is too dangerous to inspect.

In the following section, a diagram of the property is labeled with codes from both charts. The findings are explained in detail in the pages after the diagram.

Part III: Diagram and explanation of findings

Inspectors show a lot of individual style when it comes to completing this section of the report. This could be a gold mine for anyone making a psychological study of the pest control industry—but it's usually a frustrating maze for homeowners or buyers who are trying to figure out why they're paying thousands of dollars for repairs. The style you see here is one of the clearest of those commonly seen.

The diagram is a floor plan, including porches, stairs, abutments, and garages of the inspected house. The inspector draws the outlines of the house as if you were looking straight down from above and adds in major structural divisions. In the

sample diagram, the porch, garage, front steps and abutments are distinguished from the central structure. Inspectors seldom indicate where rooms are and seldom draw separate floor plans for each story in a home.

If yours is a limited report, the inspector only draws the inspected areas. If the report is limited to the substructure, for example, the diagram leaves out features like front steps, porches and garages. The inspector is responsible for reporting any problems found in diagramed areas.

The inspector marks infested or structurally unsound areas with the appropriate number from the section above. If one area has several problems, the inspector denotes the first problem with an A, the second with a B, etcetera. The inspector has written the number 4, for example, on the diagram wherever there are porches or steps with structural infestation or damage. Since the model home's porches have problems in several distinct areas, the diagram is marked with the codes 4A, 4B and 4C. These codes refer the reader to particular paragraphs on the following pages.

Inspectors may also add letter codes from the chart above to show what kinds of problems they

The owners of this house were sitting in their living room when they heard a loud crash in the front yard. Outside, they found the front steps crumbled on the ground. Fungi had eaten away the wood structural support underneath until nothing was left but the concrete surface. Regular maintenance inspections by an experienced operator, however, could have discovered the problem earlier, when the steps might still have been salvaged.

Inspectors should note in the report any problems with windows and make recommendations for their correction. Moisture often condenses in window corners and encourages decay, as it has done here.

found in the marked areas, as you see in the sample diagram. An F placed next to 4A indicates that there is fungus damage in this area. The problem will be explained further in the paragraphs below. The number codes and letter itemizations for areas are circled to distinguish them from the letter codes for problems. Otherwise, you could easily confuse 1A (substructure area, first problem) with IA (inaccessible areas).

The inspector explains his findings in paragraphs arranged by area and recommends repair and treatment for each problem. Under "Porches" for example, you read that the area labeled 4A—the stairs along the side of the garage—has fungus damage in the landing, steps and structural support, and will require rebuilding. The "Other" area (labeled 9 on the diagram) includes problems from the many parts of a house that don't fit into any of the preceding categories—such as roofs, windows and doors, and support posts. Of course, categorization varies between inspectors.

Recommendations are usually completed by the pest control operator. They're what the operator bases the repair bid on. Occasionally, however, inspectors make recommendations for the homeowner to do some simple fix-ups. These recommendations don't figure into the cost of repairs. In paragraph 1A, for example, the owner is asked to move shelves stored on the earth floor. If a homeowner intends to have a contractor without a pest control license perform repairs, the contractor will make a bid and work according to the operator's recommendations.

Operators don't always describe in full the repairs that a pest-damaged or structurally defective area might need. It's common practice for operators to refer homeowners to specialized contractors when problems are suspected in the roof or plumbing. Inspectors are only required to report the condition of the part of a roof they can see from ground level—often no more than the gutter. Hence, an inspector may report that leaks in a roof and gutter have caused fungus damage, but may leave repair of the roof and gutter up to a roofer. Similarly, inspectors aren't required to inspect or repair plumbing, even though leaks often lead to excessive moisture conditions and damage. If an inspector notices a leak during inspection of the house, the inspector may report it and correct any fungus-damaged wood, but may leave the plumbing repairs to a plumber.

The specialized design of roofs and plumbing may make this referral practice reasonable for problems in those areas. Yet when the practice is extended to easily inspected areas, the homeowner's interests are being betrayed. When operators leave inspection and repair to other contractors, homeowners have no guarantee that all structural pest damage will be discovered and removed. Operators should make recommendations for repair and treatment as specific as possible.

One example of misuse of the referral practice is a recommendation for the homeowner to "contact a licensed window contractor to make necessary repairs and corrections." A report can thus acknowledge that windows are decayed, but it doesn't say which windows are infested or how much repairs will cost. Furthermore, the findings of this inspection and the bid for repair can't be checked against those of another inspection which would include window repairs.

Some operators tend to produce poorly drawn diagrams and vaguely written paragraphs. This makes it difficult for contractors to bid from the report or for homeowners to do the work themselves—or even to use the report to examine the building. Such reports may also complicate attempts to prove an operator liable for missed infestations or conditions. You may not be able to hold an operator liable for a missed infestation if the operator's findings are so vaguely written that you can't tell what he was identifying or where.

One reason why many reports are vague or difficult to read is the misuse of codes. In the model home's report, the area codes introduced in Part II are used consistently to label the diagram and paragraphs in Part III. Sometimes, though, inspectors simply number paragraphs sequentially, so that these numbers have no relation to the nine structural areas in Part II. Many inspectors omit letter codes from the diagram entirely.

Upon completion of an inspection, the operator hangs a dated inspection tag in the attic, subarea or garage. The report must indicate the location of that tag and of any other tags on the property less than two years old. This alerts homeowners and buyers to earlier reports which are on file with the Structural Pest Control Board.

Disclaimer

Pest control operators usually write a disclaimer in the beginning of Part III or at the end of the inspection report. The content of the disclaimer varies greatly between inspectors, but it may exempt the operator from liability for repairs and treatments that the homeowner doesn't complete through that operator.

In addition, many disclaimers state that certain areas of houses are inaccessible for inspection and that the operator assumes no liability for damage or conditions subsequently discovered there. Typically inaccessible areas include paneled basement walls, stucco-sided walls and other wood structures with finished surfaces. The disclaimer is often the only statement that lets you know these areas have been excluded from the report. (Areas which are inaccessible in the inspected home, but which are typically accessible, should have been labeled "IA" on the diagram). If the inspector has reason to suspect that a problem exists in an inaccessible area, the "FI" box in Part II should be checked and a recommendation should be made to open these areas up for further inspection.

Inspectors call an area "inaccessible" if the area is typically inspected but cannot be reached because of an unusual obstacle. This subarea, for example, is inaccessible because dirt is piled high against the joists. Inspectors may recommend that the area be cleared for further inspection.

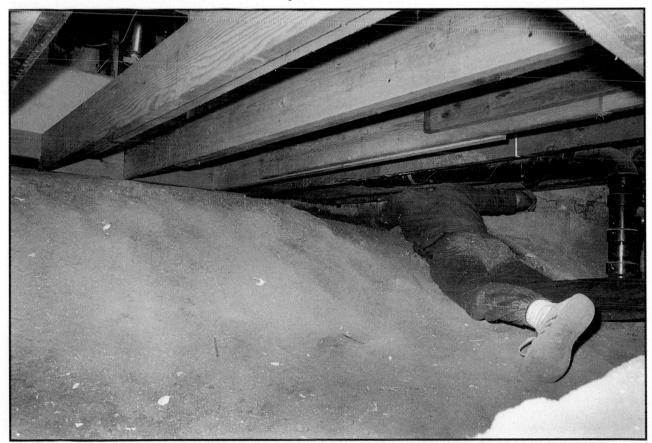

Beware of reports that leave out vulnerable areas of your home by labeling them inaccessible without recommending further inspection. Some areas may be very inconvenient to inspect, but not truly inaccessible. Attics, for example, are often labeled inaccessible when they are physically strenuous to inspect. If the house is in a locale plagued by drywood termites, attic inspection is worth the extra effort. If the house is in an area where inspectors never see drywood termites, then it probably isn't efficient to check the attic. If there is no attic access opening at all, inspectors should recommend that you have one made.

Two stories of this stucco house (left) rest on a mudsill at the bottom of a hill. The mudsill passed an inspection just before the house was sold. It was subsequently discovered that the sill was so rotted that it was almost hollow —so the weight of the house rests on little more than splinters (right). Rainwater had leaked from the windows and deck down behind the stucco siding and collected in the sill. Operators may be liable for repairing such missed infestations.

Most disclaimers include a statement that guarantees the operator's work for a limited period of time (one year for most work in the case of the sample report). In some states, however, homeowners have protection against incomplete or improper work beyond the warranty period. In California, the Pest Control Board will review a complaint as long as the report is still on file—two years. Courts may hear cases concerning less recent inspections.

Often, operators exempt themselves from liability for new infestations or conditions that arise after they have certified a home to be free of these problems. Again, a state board (like California's) may hold operators liable for infestations discovered in areas they inspected up to two years after completion of the work. If a homeowner receives a report of new infestation during this time, the homeowner may file a complaint with the board.

If the board enters the dispute, it could make one of several judgments on the case:

1) An infestation, present at the time of the original inspection, was missed by the inspector.

2) A condition, present at the time of the original inspection, was missed and subsequently led to infestation.

3) Treatment for an infestation found at the time of the original inspection was inadequate and failed to stop the progress of the infestation.

4) Workmanship on repair work was inadequate and led to further infestation.

5) A new infestation or condition occurred that could not have been anticipated by the inspector.

The case is most often one of the first four. A new infestation is unlikely to cause costly damage to a sound home in less than two years.

If the board judges that the case is one of the first four, the operator performing the original inspection may be liable and would probably be required to repair the damage at his own cost. In the last case, the homeowner pays for repairs and treatment.

In California, a notice is printed at the bottom of the report that any interested party may receive a copy of the report within two years by sending $2 to the Structural Pest Control Board.

Contract and Work Authorization Form

The structural pest control report is usually accompanied by a contract and work authorization form that itemizes the cost of repairs to be performed by the operator and sets the terms of the contract. The terms may include a deadline for signing the authorization, request for payment in full upon completion of work or progress payments during work, provisions for installing smoke detectors if the cost of repairs exceeds $1,000, and a waiver of responsibility for construction defects unrelated to wood-destroying pests and for additional work not specified in the report.

In California, the contract may also include a statement about the mechanic lien law. This law gives operators and contractors the right to enforce a claim against your property if you don't pay everyone who worked there in full. To preserve their rights under this law, contractors should give you a "preliminary notice" that lists who has the right to file a claim against you in case you fail to pay. The notice is not the same as a claim. If a contractor files a claim and a court hearing supports the claim, the court could sell your home to pay your debts.

If the operator's work is performed as part of a real estate transaction, the contract requires signatures of both the buyer and the seller and their agents. The contract should also specify the address of the property, the name of the inspector, the inspector's license number, the title company and escrow number for the sale, and, if there is no escrow, the name of the party who the operator should bill.

Standard Notice of Work Completed and Not Completed

Upon completion of the work specified in the contract, the operator provides the Structural Pest Control Board, the homeowner, and other interested parties with copies of the "Standard Notice of Work Completed and Not Completed." Usually, most of the operator's recommendations will have been completed unless the operator referred the homeowner or buyer to another contractor for work requiring unusual expertise or unless the homeowner made provisions for someone else to do some of the work.

Standard Notice of Work Completed and Not Completed

NOTICE - All recommendations may not have been completed. - See below - Recommendations not completed. This form is prescribed by the Structural Pest Control Board, with whom a copy must be filed by license within 5 days after completion of work under a contract.

THIS IS A NOTICE OF COMPLETION ONLY, NOT AN INSPECTION REPORT.

ADDRESS OF PROPERTY INSPECTED:	BLDG. NO. 2001	STREET Maple Street	CITY: Anytown CO. CODE 01	DATE OF COMPLETION: 6-30-88

A-TERMITE Control
125 Main Street
Anytown, USA   00000-0000   (003) 555-7000

MEMBER PEST CONTROL ASSOCIATION

AFFIX STAMP TO BOARD COPY ONLY

FIRM LICENSE NUMBER: 1234	COMPLETION STAMP NUMBER: 976844Z

Notice of Completion .... Sherry Nordstrom, Sure-Sale Realty 4000 Pleasant Dr., Anytown, USA
Sent To and Date: 6-30-88

Owner's Name and Address: Leah Cordova, 2001 Maple St., Anytown, USA
Copies Sent To: Above.

This is to certify that the following recommendations on the above designated property, as outlined in STANDARD INSPECTION REPORT NO. 127986A dated 6-14-88, REGISTRATION STAMP NO. 127986A, have been and/or have not been completed. SUPPLEMENTAL REPORT, State Stamp No. 127990A, 6-17-88.

Recommendations completed that are in accordance with the Structural Pest Control Board's Rules and Regulations:

ITEMS: 1B, 1C, 1D, 1E, 1F, 1G, 2B, 2C, 3A, 3B, 3C, 4A, 4B, 4C, 5A, 6A, 6B, 6C, 7A, 7B, 7C, 7E, 8A, 9A, 9B, 9C, 9D, and 9E.
ITEMS: 1A, 2A, and 7D are information only.

Recommendations completed that are considered secondary measures under Section 1992 of the Structural Pest Control Board's Rules and Regulations:

None.

Cost: $	7,000.00
Inspection Fee: $	Paid
Other: $	
Total: $	7,000.00

Recommendations not completed by this firm:

ITEM: 1A has been completed by the owner.

Estimated Cost: $

Remarks: This is to certify that the property described herein is now free of evidence of active infestation or infection as outlined by the State of California Structural Pest Control Laws and Regulations. This certification includes the visible/accessible areas only.
The chemical Dursban TC was applied to the soil in the subarea and Copper Naphthenates was applied to the wood members.
A-TERMITE Control Completion tag is located on the subarea framing.
This Notice of Completion is intended to become part of and attached to A-TERMITE Control ORIGINAL REPORT, State Stamp No. 127986A, 6-14-88 and SUPPLEMENTAL REPORT, State Stamp No. 127990A, 6-17-88.

Signature _____

If you have questions regarding the work as outlined above, you should first contact the licensee noted above. If satisfaction is not obtained you may contact the Structural Pest Control Board at:

Los Angeles - 213-620-2255
Sacramento - 916-920-6323
San Francisco -415-557-9114

You are entitled to obtain copies of all reports and completion notices on this property filed with the Board during the preceding two years upon payment of a $2.00 search fee to: The Structural Pest Control Board, 1430 Howe Ave., Sacramento, California 95825.

In certain cases, the homeowner or buyer may need certification that the home is pest-free. For example, a financial institution may not grant a mortgage until the home receives pest-free certification. Only operators licensed for structural pest control may provide this. If the home has no evidence of active infestation when it's inspected, certification is given in the inspection report. If the operator had to repair or treat the home, the "Standard Notice of Work Completed and Not Completed" provides pest-free certification by specifying that the operator has completed all the recommended work. If the operator's recommendations were completed by a contractor without a pest control license or by the homeowner, the home can only be certified when a licensed operator reinspects it (as is done in the reinspection report in Appendix 3). No notice of completion is given in this last case.

Certification usually means that a home is free of evidence of active infestation. If an operator does not remove all of the reported infestations, the certification must describe the infestations that remain. Be aware that operators may certify a home that has conditions conducive to infestation as long as it is free of pests and fungi. For example, a home with faulty grade may be certified as long as the faulty grade has not encouraged infestation.

Chapter 7

Transacting a Sale

Most structural pest control inspections are ordered in connection with the sale of real estate. The results of an inspection can significantly affect the terms under which you buy or sell a home. The report can mean thousands of dollars of gain or loss for one side or the other in a transaction, depending on the terms of the sale. Because the stakes are so high, it's important to look closely at the options and pitfalls which affect buyers, sellers and realtors.

Who will pay?

One of the most difficult points to determine in a transaction is who should take financial responsi-bility for pest control inspection and repair. In some parts of the country, it is customary for the seller to pay all costs. Elsewhere, it's common to sell a house "as is." The house's selling price has the greatest influence on this question—so each transaction must be negotiated differently.

Often, the buyer pays for inspection of all accessible areas of the house—including attached structures such as decks, garages, fences, etc. The seller agrees to bear the repair costs of all existing damage revealed in the report. The buyer may pay for correction of problem conditions that have not yet caused damage, although the responsibility for this is open to negotiation. The buyer also decides

Homebuyers have many different versions of what a home should be. But many will share similar experiences with financial compromises and structural pest certification before a real home becomes their own.

Stucco abutments may look solid (left), but often hide serious infestations (right). They should be included in an inspection when a home is sold. Buyers and sellers should decide how to pay for this part of the inspection. The seller, for example, could pay for pest control work if damage is found in the abutment, while the buyer could cover the costs of opening and repairing the abutment if it has no problems.

whether to have inaccessible areas inspected. If no structural pest damage is found in these areas once they're opened up, the buyer should pay for the additional inspection and the cost of reassembly of these areas. If damage is found, the seller should pay for inspection and reassembly. In any case, buyer and seller should agree on the extent of each party's responsibility and write this agreement into the real estate contract before it is delivered to the escrow officer.

If the contract specifies an agreement in which the seller agrees to pay for some or all of the repair, funds sufficient to cover the cost of repair are usually subtracted from the proceeds of the sale and held in escrow until work is completed by a contrac-

tor. Usually, the contractor is then paid directly from the escrow account. The buyer never sees the funds, has no direct control over their dispersal, and has no contractual obligations to the contractor. If the buyer has agreed to pay part of the repair costs, the buyer's mortgage lender may require the buyer to place enough funds in the escrow account to cover the buyer's share of the bill. This insures that work won't be left unfinished after the buyer assumes possession of the house.

If the home is one of the few sold "as is"—with the buyer assuming all repair obligations—the buyer's mortgage lender may require the buyer to place, in escrow, funds that are as much as double the amount of the pest control operator's repair estimate. This is especially troublesome, however, because buyers who prefer the "as is" home purchase often operate with minimum capital. They may not have sufficient funds to place the full amount for repair in escrow and to complete the deal on the house. If buyers plan to do the work themselves—which might save 30 to 60 percent of the repair estimate—this requirement ties up the money needed as day-to-day working capital for the project. Funds for this purpose can be disbursed from the escrow account, but the procedure is awkward and slow. Usually, the escrow officer or bank will permit disbursement only upon certification that the entire home is free of structural pest problems.

When the seller places a dollar or percentage limit on the amount of repairs for which the seller will pay, prospective buyers should examine the entire pest control report carefully, calculate the remainder of the repair bill, and decide whether to hold firm on the original offer, submit a lower offer or withdraw from the deal altogether. Occassionally, a seller will agree to pay for all repairs except those needed on a deck or garage. This often happens because the seller knows there are problems with these areas, has adjusted the price accordingly and doesn't want a prospective buyer to use those items as a basis for further price negotiation.

In any case, the crucial issue is the house's selling price. Any arrangement for repair of structural pest damage may be reasonable, depending on the price of the house.

The "as is" home

Sometimes, the "as is" home is the best arrangement for both seller and buyer. In this case, the house changes hands without a structural pest clearance. Occassionally, an "as is" sale may even be made without a pest control report—but this is a risky situation and should be avoided.

An "as is" seller doesn't need to deal with the problems of repair work, and the buyer—if the mortgage lender approves this arrangement—usually pays a lower price for the home. An "as is" house offers financial advantages, but it may not suit the attitudes of many homebuyers. Most of us become uneasy at the very thought that our present or future house may be infested. We may panic at the discovery of an infestation and we may want to take swift, firm action against it.

Others, however, can accept a structural pest problem just as they'd accept an old, well-worn

automobile that will need an overhaul or replacement parts eventually, but adequately serves its purpose for the moment. For these homeowners or home buyers, an infestation or problem condition is something to monitor in case things take a turn for the worse. In a few cases, a condition may be left as it is for years without causing structural damage. Sometimes redwood mudsills in contact with the earth can give useful service for 15 to 20 years without conducting fungi to other parts of a home. A lucky owner might get away without replacing the mudsills until years after the damage is discovered. This is not recommended, however. Homeowners in earthquake-prone areas, in particular, should never risk the structural integrity of their house.

Seller's view

Except for times when a buyer agrees to purchase a home "as is", the seller of the home is usually responsible for some or all pest control work. All too often, sellers feel that this responsibility is a financial dead end. Homeowners could find that they

This house was bought as-is for $80,000 in a neighborhood where most houses sell for $150,000. The buyer knew it had extensive structural damage, especially in the corners decayed by leaking downspouts (left). The buyer has removed the stucco siding (above) and will replace much of the wood framing—at a cost of $40,000 to $60,000. The cost of the house and repairs will add up to less than the cost of a home with a clear report.

actually have several options for fulfilling their end of the deal—if they order pest control inspections early in the process of planning a sale. More often than not, a buyer's mortgage lender will require a pest control inspection before approving a loan. The seller will have to reckon with the results of the inspection sooner or later, and it's to the seller's advantage to do so sooner. Before the home goes up for sale, the seller should sit down with a realtor for a market analysis and estimate what the proceeds of the sale are likely to be after deducting the real estate commission, closing costs and the cost of structural pest control work. The accuracy of this estimate is especially important if the seller intends to use the proceeds as a down payment on another home.

If the inspection shows that your house needs substantial repair work, let your agent help you think through your marketing options. You may, for example, want to set a limit on how much you will pay for repairs or you may want to sell the home "as is" and lower the asking price. In any case, you should estimate the proceeds under several options.

The stucco home next door may need similar repairs if it has structural defects—such as a leaky roof, unprotected rafter ends or plumbing leaks—that keep the walls and floors damp.

The seller who chooses to complete repairs before the sale—and thus increase the value of the house—has several options also. You may have the operator of your choice complete repairs and certify the home. You may do the repair work suggested in the initial inspection report yourself or have it done by a contractor who isn't a licensed pest control operator, then obtain another inspection report and certification. Such contractors can occasionally complete repairs for much less than the amount of the bid in the initial report. Where permitted by law, and when the work conforms to local building codes and pest control practices, this strategy is economical for the seller and fair to the buyer. Its one drawback, however, is that it can make the process of obtaining final certification from a pest control operator more difficult.

Sellers may occasionally be tempted to try two other strategies when the initial report is unfavorable. A seller might shop around for an inspection from another company whose standards are lower than the first and who will send an inspector likely to see fewer problems—known in the industry as "the best blind inspector." A seller might also limit subsequent reports to the substructure only—eliminating problem areas such as the roof, windows, and fences.

If you genuinely believe that the repair estimate you received is inflated or unfair, discuss the possibility of obtaining a second inspection and repair bid with your realtor. Remember that some states do require that prospective buyers be given access to all current reports. Some buyers may insist, as part of the offer, on choosing the pest control operator who inspects the home. They may also insist that the inspection include all areas of your home—especially if they've read this book.

If you're considering selling your home in the future, inspect it every one and one half years and correct problem conditions promptly. Follow the inspection guideline in Chapter 5. Many conditions that contribute to pest infestation are easily corrected at comparatively little expense if you have the time and energy to do them yourself. Repeating this maintenance process regularly increases the chances that your house will get a clean bill of health at its first structural pest inspection.

Buyer's view

The accuracy and detail of an inspection report are more important for the buyer than is the timing of the report. As a buyer, you have the options of accepting a current structural pest report already on file (ordered by the seller or another prospective

Homeowners can preserve the value of their houses and avoid costly repairs without investing much money by doing regular maintenance, such as cleaning out gutters. There's no excuse for letting gutters become planter boxes like this one.

If areas covered by fancy woodwork—like this detailed siding—need structural repairs, make sure that the operator chosen to do the work can restore the details to their original quality.

buyer), ordering further inspection by the company that filed the original report or ordering a new report from a pest control operator of your choice. Before you accept a report already on file, consider the reputation of the company and the completeness of the report carefully.

You should be convinced that the company that made the existing report is stable enough financially to back it up. In California, operators are indemnified by a $4,000 bond. If a consumer had a claim against the operator greater than that amount (or, worse still, if other dissatisfied customers had already filed claims), the company could go bankrupt and have its license revoked. In that case, the consumer would be left without further recourse against the operator. If, on the other hand, a company does three million dollars worth of repair work annually in your state, that operator can be responsible for claims well in excess of the bond amount.

Make sure the operator can do repair work that is equal to the quality of the building. Drive by other homes repaired by the operator to see how well stucco patterns match, wood details conform, etc.

It's important to check up on the operator even when the seller agrees to bear all the repair costs. If there are problems with the report or repair work that turn up after you have possession of the home, you'll be the one to file a claim against the company. If you're not happy with what you learn about the company, it may be worthwhile to find another (possibly more expensive) operator—even if you have to pay for the difference. In the long run, there's no substitute for quality work.

Make sure the existing structural pest report is as complete as possible. Homes are often sold with a notice of completion stating that all known damage and problem conditions have been repaired. The notice of completion, however, may be based on a structural pest report that excludes specific areas from inspection. The pest control operator may be exempt from liability should damage be discovered in any of these excluded areas.

There is seldom a good reason for you to accept a report that is limited to the substructure. Repair costs for decayed doors, windows, gutters, soffets, roofs, siding, and the areas around sinks, tubs, showers, toilets and furnaces can far exceed the costs of foundation repairs and chemical treatment.

Structures attached to the house such as decks, garages, and fences or out-of-the-way areas such as attics may be excluded from an inspection report because the seller ordered their exclusion or because

Reports that are limited to the substructure don't tell you anything about problems with features like this inset gutter, which could be leaking water behind the stucco siding. Make sure you see a complete report before you agree to buy a house.

Inaccessible areas—those which cannot be inspected without partially dismantling or causing damage to finished surfaces—can be difficult to choose to inspect. It's important to weigh the cost of inspection and reassembly of such areas against the cost of repair if any infestation is found there. If, for example, it costs $150 to inspect and repair a paneled basement wall and if the maximum damage likely to be revealed there is $1,000, the additional inspection probably isn't worth the cost unless the pest control operator has a specific reason to suspect concealed damage. If that $150 inspection reveals $10,000 worth of damage, on the other hand, ordering the additional inspection becomes harder to resist. You should discuss your choices in these situations with the pest control operator. If, before the initial inspection, you already suspect that there is damage in an inaccessible area, arrange with the seller to make it accessible before the operator arrives. This can save the expense of a second inspection. If the home that interests you has already been inspected and the report calls for further inspection, do it—even if you must bear the additional cost.

Access to a complete structural pest report is important even when buying a home "as is," although the actual repair work suggested in the report may not be completed until long after the home has changed hands or may not be performed by the operator who made the original report. All too often, however, the buyer of an "as is" home is ignorant of the structural condition of the property and assumes that everything is in order. A structural pest report may never have been ordered or an existing report may never have been made available to the buyer. The financial risks of buying a home under these circumstances are exceedingly high. An inspection of the house—which costs about $150—might reveal $5,000 to $10,000 worth of repair work that is invisible to the untrained observer. If you purchase a home "as is," make sure you know what its "as is" condition is!

For many buyers, the benefits of an "as is" home can outweigh the risks—as long as the buyers have been able to examine an acceptably completed structural pest report. Besides its lower price, the "as is" home offers buyers the advantage of deciding how, when, and by whom repairs are to be completed. For example, a buyer might apply money saved by buying "as is" to a renovation that includes infested areas, instead of simply repairing the damage there. If cash flow is a problem, the buyer may decide to do the repairs over a protracted period of time or hire someone else as money becomes

their exclusion is standard practice in that state. You should have these features inspected not only because of the potential cost of repairing them, but because they often serve as conduits for pests to enter other areas of the home. In addition, these areas can be the only visible entry point for otherwise undetectable infestations.

Detached structures such as wooden greenhouses, pool cabanas, free-standing fences and garages don't represent the same danger to the house as attached structures do. However, repair costs for these structures can still be great. If any of these features contribute significantly to the home's market value, it's probably worthwhile to include them in the report. For example, if you believe that an attractive, apparently sound garage contributes $15,000 to the price of the home and if you don't plan to tear it down to make room for a swimming pool, you probably ought to have it inspected.

available. In an inflationary housing market, a homeowner may decide to defer repairs until the property is resold and then pay for the work with the realized profit. Alternatively, the homeowner may resell the home "as is" and let the new owner decide what to do about the repairs.

If you buy a home "as is" or enter into a contract where you agree to bear part of the repair costs, reach an understanding with your mortgage lender about any funds to be held in escrow before you make a final decision to go with that lender. Shop around for better terms if that lender's escrow requirements interfere with your repair or renovation plans.

Agent's view

The real estate agent's role in any home sale is to assist the client in negotiating the sale as efficiently and thoroughly as possible. Agents can be extremely helpful to buyers and sellers because of their experience in judging the value of a home on the basis of qualified inspectors' assessments of the home's condition. In addition, realtors can inform clients of options for inspecting and repairing a home. They should discuss the problems raised earlier in this chapter, such as limited reports, exempted areas, detached structures and limits on responsibility for repair costs.

Most real estate agents try to give a complete and honest representation of the structural integrity of the home under consideration. To be assured of the value of a home, clients often need more information than is provided by the termite report. Agents can refer clients to contractors who have the expertise to give an opinion on a particular feature or to prepare a supplemental report on a home's condition.

Circumstances sometimes arise that complicate the realtor's job. If a seller has ordered several structural pest reports, it's important for both the seller's and the buyer's realtors to obtain copies of all current reports, even if state law doesn't require that such reports be made available. If important information from any one of these reports is withheld from the buyer, both realtors could find themselves in court as defendants in a civil lawsuit for misrepresentation that results in punitive or financial damages. If either realtor suspects that the seller has concealed structural damage, the agent should pursue the matter (perhaps with the help of the agency's business lawyer) and disclose all pertinent facts. In California, the law holds sellers, as well as realtors, liable for hiding structural problems.

If realtors or sellers are found guilty of hiding structural damage, a court could hold them responsible for more than the cost of repairs. In 1982, a California couple won a judgment against a broker for $81,800, which included $30,000 in punitive damages and damages for emotional distress. The couple bought a house said to be in "good condition" in the broker's listings. The broker gave both the sellers and buyers a structural pest report showing faulty grade level and fungus damage, but withheld a second report indicating extensive termite damage. Ultimately, the house was found to be in such bad condition that the cost of repairs would have exceeded the value of the house.

The intention of most agents is to satisfy all parties' needs for accurate and detailed information so that sales can be transacted smoothly. Buyers and sellers should realize, however, that agents can only assume the responsibility of disclosing known details. They aren't responsible for preparing reports on a home's condition themselves. Buyers and sellers should take an active role in gathering complete information by contacting qualified inspectors.

Chapter 8

The Lesser Evil

You want to protect your home from the structural and economic threat of termites and other pests. You also want to protect your family from chemical health hazards. Knowing what kinds and quantities of pesticides are safe for your home is just as crucial as knowing the financial ins-and-outs of pest control work.

In California, pest control operators are required to alert homeowners and tenants to the importance of the proper use of pesticides with this statement:

"State law requires that you be given the following information: CAUTION— PESTICIDES ARE TOXIC CHEMICALS. Structural pest control operators are licensed and regulated by the Structural Pest Control Board, and apply pesticides which are registered and approved for use by the California Department of Food and Agriculture and by the United States Environmental Protection Agency. Registration is granted when the state finds that based on existing scientific evidence there are no appreciable risks if proper use conditions are followed or that the risks are outweighed by the benefits. The degree of risk depends upon the degree of exposure, so exposure should be minimized."

"If within 24 hours following application you experience symptoms similar to common seasonal illness comparable to the flu, contact your physician or poison control center and your pest control operator immediately."

The statement must end with the phone numbers of the poison control center, pest control operator, County Health Department, County Agricultural Commissioner and the Structural Pest Control Board.

Many other states require similar warnings. The risks of pesticide treatments are taken seriously by officials and professionals everywhere, and need to be given careful consideration by homeowners as well. While pest control operators have the knowledge to prescribe chemical pesticide treatments, you should decide whether or not to allow use of pesticides in your home. This decision can be a difficult one to make. Few homeowners can stand idly by while the emotional and financial investments in their home are silently eaten away by organisms that are barely visible. Unfortunately, the only available method of controlling these organisms—if solid home design and careful maintenance can't stop them—involves the use of chemicals that can harm people as well as the pests they're meant to destroy. Structural pesticides must be toxic enough to kill relatively simple and vigorous organisms in small, hidden places. In many situations, the chemical agent must last long enough for the residue from the original application to check infestation for months or years afterwards. These qualities of an effective pesticide all but guarantee additional harm to humans.

Most chemicals used by the pest control industry fall into three categories: soil termiticides, fumigants and fungicides. Soil termiticides include several families of chemicals applied against subterranean termites: chlorinated hydrocarbons such as chlordane (most of which have been banned); organophosphates such as chlorpyrifos and isofenphos; and pyrethroids such as permethrin, fenvalerate and cypermethrin. Fumigants are chemicals applied against drywood termites and beetles: mainly sulfuryl flouride and methyl bromide.

Fungicides are applied to wood to prevent fungus infections. Wood is soaked under pressure—"pressure-treated"—at lumberyards with inorganic arsenic compounds ("arsenicals"), pentachlorophenol (a chlorinated hydrocarbon) or copper-based compounds. The fungicides that contain copper are the least highly toxic. Copper napthenate is available to the public through hardware and building stores.

To ensure that pesticides and fungicides are applied effectively and safely, many of them can only be purchased by specially trained and licensed operators.

Soil Termiticides

The chlorinated hydrocarbons are the oldest group of synthetic pesticides. For many years, they were also the most popular for treatment of subterranean termite infestations because their residue could provide complete protection against new infestations for decades after the original application. Chlorinated hydrocarbons—including DDT, the first to be used against insects—are very resistant to environmental breakdown. One undesirable result of their stability is their tendency to collect in the food chain and reach potentially dangerous levels in higher organisms, including people. Because of this, the EPA banned DDT in the United States in 1971.

Most of the termiticides in the chlorinated hydrocarbon family—chlordane, heptachlor, aldrin and dieldrin could only be applied to the soil around the perimeter of an infested house, near the foundation. This is known as the "trench-and-treat" method or subterranean ground insertion. Recently, the EPA decided that this application restriction didn't go far enough to protect people from toxic residues. The EPA banned the use of most forms of these chemicals in 1988. Chlordane, however, is still available under several brand names for private use by homeowners. Lindane, another family member, and pentachlorophenol are widely available. A newly-developed relative, endosulfan, is gaining popularity in the industry.

Subterranean ground insertion is still the standard method of applying chemicals against subterranean termites. Since the ban on chlordane, the most commonly used termiticides have been chloropyrifos, an organophosphate, and permethrin, a synthetic pyrethroid. Neither of these chemicals provides as stable a barrier against termite infestations as does chlordane. Depending on environmental conditions, they may be effective for as few as five to as many as 20 years. Because organophosphates and pyrethroids break down more quickly than the chlorinated hydrocarbons, it's assumed

that they pose less of a threat of long-term toxicity. The EPA continues to test these relatively new chemicals.

Another termiticide being tested by researchers is sodium borate salt, or borax. Though a few exterminators claim outstanding results from this common household chemical, it has not yet won approval from state and federal agencies.

Fumigants

The other class of widely used insecticides is the fumigants. These compounds vaporize at low temperatures and produce a toxic concentration of gas that kills all animal life confined in the area where the gas is released. Fumigants can be applied in liquid, gas, or even solid form. Operators favor fumigants that will penetrate into cracks and wood surfaces. Because of the fumigants' penetrating ability and toxicity, buildings are usually "tented" with large tarpaulins. The tarps are held to the ground at the corners with large clamps and along the sides with sand-filled bags (called "snakes") that go around the perimeter of the house.

After the home is tented and the foreman has personally walked through all of the rooms (including the basement and attic, if accessible) to make sure that no people, pets or stray animals—other than termites or beetles—remain in the house, workers release a measured amount of gas and quickly close the last seam of the tent. Warning signs are posted along the sides of the home. Although fumigants are released in deadly concentrations in the tents, these gases dissipate quickly once the tent is removed. Because fumigants have no residual effect, the house is subject to reinfestation immediately after the tent is removed, unless vulnerable wood has been pressure-treated.

The fumigants in general use have changed in recent years. Few operators use hydrogen cyanide today. Only two fumigants are widely used for structural pest control—methyl bromide and sulfuryl flouride.

Methyl bromide is an extremely toxic substance with excellent penetrating properties. In its gaseous state, it's three times heavier than air. Because it has very little odor, a warning gas such as tear gas (chloropicrin) is mixed in with the pesticide. Methyl bromide is less damaging to plants than other fumigants. In fact, it's used to fumigate some agricultural products. Methyl bromide kills insects slowly. It sometimes takes five or six days after fumigation for the insects to expire. Yet, unlike sul-

Fumigants are released inside tented houses in concentrations that kill all animal life within. Operators fumigate a home when they find signs of drywood termite and beetle infestations. Often, however, these signs are left by long-departed colonies. Homeowners should encourage inspectors to double-check homes for active infestations before contracting for a costly fumigation.

furyl flouride, it is toxic to all stages of insect life.

One major disadvantage of methyl bromide is that it produces a vile-smelling residual odor when it reacts with materials in the house that contain sulfur (including rubber, leather, and animal hair). In homes with wall-to-wall carpeting, the padding and any wool carpets must be removed before fumigation, or another fumigant must be selected. Furniture containing rubber, animal hair or leather must also be removed.

Sulfuryl flouride has fumigant properties similar to methyl bromide. It's nonflammable, colorless, odorless (and so must be used with a warning gas), and extremely toxic. It vaporizes at a lower temperature and is slightly heavier than methyl bromide. Because of this, it can be used at lower temperatures than other fumigants. Its penetrating action is even better than that of methyl bromide, and it doesn't leave unpleasant odors. Unfortunately, it's a much more expensive gas to produce. Consequently, it's used only in circumstances where its convenience, penetrating ability and low-temperature vaporizing qualities justify the additional expense.

Hydrogen cyanide is used in a few areas as a fumigant, but its handling properties are extremely hazardous and its penetrating action is poor. It's colorless as a gas, and is available compressed in liquid form or as a liquid-impregnated fibrous material. Often, operators create the gas at the fumigation site by placing sodium cyanide "eggs" in sulfuric acid. Hydrogen cyanide vaporizes at a relatively high temperature and is slightly lighter than air. What makes hydrogen cyanide especially dangerous is that it requires some sort of heating device to speed vapor formation—and as the volume of gas increases, so does its flammability.

Because fumigants kill all animal life trapped within a tented house and could seriously harm people or pets nearby if the tent opened up, operators must use considerable skill and care while tenting a home and injecting a fumigant. California requires that operators have a special license (Branch 1 Pest Control: Fumigation) to perform fumigation. Operators without this license subcontract the work to a company that holds one. In addition, many communities require that fumigators report their activities to the local fire department (which may require another special permit). Some communities prohibit the use of hydrogen cyanide. An increasing number of communities require a trained guard equipped with a protective mask and safety kit to be on hand at all times during the day or two that the home is tented, until the home is opened up and the gas dissipates in the atmosphere.

How toxic are they?

A small amount of any one of the soil termiticides or fumigants taken orally, inhaled or absorbed through skin can cause serious—perhaps fatal—damage to a body's systems. Fumigants, for example, are used in concentrations about 100 times stronger than needed to kill humans rapidly, and several breathfuls of any of them will kill an adult person.

The acute toxicity of a chemical compound is the dosage, in liquid or gas form, that will kill 50 percent of a sample population immediately. Toxicity is measured in grams of chemical per kilogram of the victim's body weight.

Stable chemicals, such as the chlorinated hydrocarbons, retain their toxicity for long periods of time. If a foundation was sprayed with chlordane five years ago, the chemical would still be active against termite infestation today. Unfortunately, it's a hazard to humans for just as long. Children who play in areas that were sprayed, or carpenters who handle or cut through treated wood while doing renovation risk exposure to residual amounts of pesticide.

Stable pesticides tend to accumulate in the environment, creating conditions of chronic (long-term) toxicity. In these conditions, pesticides can promote arteriosclerosis (hardening of the arteries), damage the immunological system or interfere with the digestion of important nutrients. The chronic toxicity of a chemical, unlike its acute toxicity, is very difficult to estimate. It may remain unknown until a great deal of the chemical accumulates in the environment, exposing people and animals to small but frequent doses.

The EPA ocassionally ventures an estimate of a chemical's long-term health hazards. Recently, a major chemical manufacturer monitored the air in homes properly treated with chlordane and presented the data to the EPA. The EPA found the level of chlordane in some types of houses to be uncomfortably high. The EPA projects that residents exposed to these levels for 70 years stand a risk of between one to three in 1,000 of developing cancer.

The EPA, recognizing the extreme toxicity of chemicals like chlordane, has subjected termiticides to increasingly stringent regulations. As you know, the EPA has banned many chlorinated hydrocarbons and limits other termiticides and fumigants to use by certified applicators.

Some homeowners didn't wait for the bad news from the EPA before taking action to protect themselves from pesticides. Some moved out of—and occasionally even destroyed—homes that received heavy termite treatments with chlordane. One homeowner on Long Island, New York was told by health officials that the air in his basement had seven times the allowable level of chlordane. He raised his house from its foundations, removed the basement and the soil surrounding it, and built a new foundation. Long Island residents with similar experiences joined together as People Against Chlordane in 1983 to lobby for a chlordane ban.

Options for protecting family and home

Ideally, we'd like to prevent infestation before chemical treatments become necessary. This requires careful home maintenance and repair of conditions that might lead to infestation. To maximize our options in the battle against structural pests, we must learn to regularly inspect for damage ourselves or bear the additional cost of frequent inspections by an operator. Correction of the problem conditions described in Chapter 5 is particularly effective against fungi and subterranean termites.

If a structural pest infestation does take hold in your home, you may still have several strategic options from which to choose. Fungus decay doesn't always require chemical treatment once it sets in. Replacing damaged wood may be more important than chemically treating it. Some pesticide experts say that fungicides are useless unless applied to pressure-treated wood. There's no sense in applying a chemical seal to wood infected within. A subterranean termite infestation leaves you chemical and non-chemical options. Drywood termites and wood-boring beetles may be the most difficult to keep out of your home, but often are only temporary visitors. Before treating a house in which inspection has revealed termite or beetle holes, make sure that the holes aren't left over from a previous infestation. Tap the suspect holes to shake out old debris and place aluminum foil under the holes. If the aluminum foil catches fresh frass, you have an active infestation on your hands. Eradication usually involves tenting and fumigation—an expensive procedure, but one that isn't likely to lead to chronic

In areas where high moisture is unavoidable, fungus-damaged wood should be replaced with pressure-treated wood. If you cut treated wood, brush or spray the cut end with a wood preservative to keep fungi from entering. Be careful when you handle treated wood—it's saturated wtih highly toxic chemicals. Wear a dust mask when sawing it. Never burn it.

Though chlordane has a high chronic toxicity, it provides no guarantee that a treated home will remain infestation-free. This termite tube has bridged a concrete foundation treated with chlordane. The tube stems from an underground colony that survived the chemical treatment.

exposure of your family to chemicals, since fumigants dissipate quickly. When a home is infested with subterranean termites, pest control operators usually recommend removal of shelter tubes (which will result in the death of any termites stranded above ground), repair of any damaged portions of the house, correction of the conditions that lead to the infestation and treatment of the soil around the foundation perimeters with pesticide. If properly applied, pesticides with high chronic toxicity usually prevent incursions into your home from underground nests that might remain intact. The use of chlordane or an equally powerful chemical to form a barrier of poisoned soil against these incursions gives pest control operators confidence that another attack is unlikely to occur in the near future, but it isn't a guarantee against reinfestation.

The non-chemical strategy calls for all of the steps above except the last. Don't treat the soil. Instead, someone (either the homeowner or an operator) should inspect the house at least once every one and a half years for signs of reinfestation, especially around the previously infested areas. The success of this strategy depends on several factors:

the structure of the house; the ability and willingness of the homeowner or operator to make frequent inspections; and the accessibility of areas that need to be inspected. The non-chemical strategy is particularly successful in homes with a full basement with unfinished walls, where it's easy to make frequent inspections and remove shelter tubes. On the other hand, homes with a slab foundation make this strategy difficult to carry out.

The non-chemical alternative is most attractive when the use of pesticides could result in harm to occupants by direct contact with the pesticide or by exposure to its vapors. Certain kinds of home construction and layout of grounds and gardening areas make contamination more likely. For example, homes with floor heaters tend to allow pesticide vapor into living areas. In some homes, vapors may collect in heavily used basements. If a house has gardens around its perimeter, there's a good chance that gardeners will be exposed to pesticides used for subsurface ground insertion.

If you decide that treatment with a non-fumigant pesticide is necessary but are concerned about its potential hazards, you might want to discuss the treatment procedure with the operator before the job begins. Find out the name of the pesticide, its concentration, and the method and location of application. You might also discuss the likelihood of problems arising from pesticide fumes. Although it's the operator's responsibility to use an approved, effective material in an appropriate manner, slip-ups do occur. An exterminating firm in California became the first in the nation to be convicted for misuse of chlordane when it sprayed a Los Angeles home to get rid of ants. Residents suffered headaches and nausea, and the firm was also ordered to consider detoxifying the home.

If you have any unanswered questions or doubts about the proposed treatment, call the state agency that has jurisdiction over matters of pesticide application or the nearest EPA office for advice.

One final suggestion: Take advantage of any opportunity to leave your home for a few days or even a few weeks after a non-fumigant treatment. If you have a vacation coming up in a month or so, postpone treatment until then. If security is not a problem in your neighborhood, plan to leave as many windows open as possible to help vapors dissipate. If ventilation in your basement is poor, have the operator make additional vents that will help fumes escape (and, at the same time, reduce the likelihood of fungus decay). If you can't leave town, see if you can arrange to stay with friends or family for a few nights. Whatever you do, try to minimize your exposure to pesticide fumes.

If someone is exposed to pesticides despite all your precautions, call a toxicologist and give first aid care as instructed in Appendix I.

Owners of homes with floor heaters, like this one, should consider using non-chemical strategies against subterranean termites. The vapor of termicides applied by subsurface ground insertion can filter into living areas through such vents.

Chapter 9

Consumer Problems

By this time, you probably realize that the complex process of controlling structural pests is fraught with potential for accidents, mistakes and negligence. This chapter explores problems that can arise during inspection, treatment or repair of a house and suggests ways to deal with them.

A pest control operator who's asked to inspect a house for infestation and recommend repair is in a situation similar to an expert mechanic who's asked to fix an old car. Even the most competent mechanic can have trouble diagnosing problems complicated by the age of the car, previous repair work by others, or idiosyncracies in the car's design. Consumers shouldn't hold the mechanic culpable if these difficulties interfere with otherwise sound work. On the other hand, consumers need not tolerate incompetent diagnosis, poor workmanship or outright fraud.

Similarly, structural pest problems aren't the fault of the operator who points them out. They've developed over the years because of poor design, careless workmanship or inadequate maintenance. Sometimes, the operator who does the most thorough inspections finds more infestation and makes higher repair estimates than would other operators. In other cases, an operator who finds evidence of an old infestation assumes the worst—without making a thorough inspection—and submits a bid that's higher than necessary.

The operator's responsibility is to diagnose your home's present condition as accurately as possible, to advise you of the advantages of supplemental inspection of inaccessible areas and, if you give the go-ahead, to repair structural damage at a price and in a manner that you approve.

Consumer complaints

If an error in inspection or repair does turn up, you need to decide whether it's the fault of the operator or of circumstances beyond the operator's control. This is a very difficult call for most homeowners to make because of the technical nature of pest control evaluation and repair. Your task will be easier if you know the consumer protection laws of your state that are pertinent to pest control. It also

This bathroom appears to be free of leaks and problems from here . . .

80

helps to know the standard practices of the industry and to have discussed the pest control procedure with the operator in advance, as outlined in earlier chapters of this book (particularly Chapter 3).

If you see evidence of structural pest activity (swarming, shelter tubes, pellets or beetle holes) within months after a pest control operator completed work, call the operator back. If the operator isn't willing to correct the problem, you may have reason to file a complaint. Although operators generally disclaim responsibility for infestations which occur after their inspection or repair work, many states hold them liable for failing to identify existing infestations and conditions that promote infestation. In these situations, it's usually best to contact the state agency that regulates pest control operators as well as the operator who performed inspection or repair work just before the new signs of infestation appeared.

If you receive an inspection report that indicates extensive damage or makes a high repair estimate for an area where little visible evidence is present, you have a suspicious situation on your hands. You may want to call another operator for a second opinion. If the two reports differ on the location and extent of infestations and conditions or if they suggest very different repairs and treatments, you might consider filing a complaint.

If you've resorted to chemical treatment of infestations in your home, another situation that could arise to provoke legal action is pesticide contamination. Recall, from Chapter 8, the exterminating company that received the nation's first criminal prosecution for misuse of chlordane after spraying the pesticide inside a home to kill ants.

Each of these situations will be discussed in detail below. If you believe there is legitimate basis for complaint, you should enlist expert help to determine whether the pest control operator is responsible for the problem. The appropriate expert in these cases is usually a state official who mediates disputes between consumers and operators. In California, the Structural Pest Control Board handles up to 2,000 complaints a year, resolves half by mediation and refers the rest to the department's investigators for possible prosecution. Officials in any state will be more responsive to your complaint if you can show a discrepancy between reports from two different operators. The state inspector will then be judging a dispute between two professionals, rather than an unequal dispute between an expert and a lay person.

... Underneath the toilet, fungi sprout around the bend and subfloor. This infestation was hidden from a pest control inspector by floor tiling above and by the basement ceiling below. It wasn't discovered until the house was remodeled. A more alert inspector might have ordered further inspection of the bathroom because of the age and construction of the house.

Inaccurate reports

Inaccurate reports are perhaps the most common cause of consumer dissatisfaction and complaint. In addition to the difficulties of diagnosing a home, the accuracy of the report may be hurt by the lack of a uniform, industry-wide system of inspection and notation. Inaccurate reports may be the cause of problems such as missed infestations and conditions, unnecessary repairs and improper pesticide treatment.

Limited inspections and reports

Operators' standard practice in California and other states with structural pest control regulations is to inspect the entire house—substructure, exterior siding, living areas, attic and roofline. Fences and other attached structures must also be included in the report.

Occasionally, the party that requests the inspection doesn't require an inspection of the entire house. A lender might only care about the substructure. A seller might prefer to keep the condition of part of a house, such as a roof, fence or deck, off the record. Deviation from the industry's standard practice is legally acceptable in these cases, as long as the scope of the inspection is clearly defined in the report. In the long run, however, a limited inspection is seldom in a homeowner's best interest. An uninspected area may harbor an active infestation that has caused thousands of dollars of damage. The infestation may eventually spread to areas that have been inspected and certified.

For example, a recent inspection of a stucco home overlooked damage worth 30 percent of the home's cost because the inspection was limited to the substructure. The necessary substructure repairs were completed by an independent contractor and, on the basis of the limited report, the home was certified to be free of infestations. The contractor, however, noticed that areas excluded from the official inspection needed extensive repair. Inset gutters and a flat-top roof had allowed water to speed decay of all wood support in the house's

The inset gutters around this older stucco house (see previous page) make the corners highly vulnerable to decay. A succession of inspectors over the years checked the corners at random and missed the rear left one (above left) each time. The most recent inspector noticed a stain on the ceiling on the inside of the corner (above right) and popped a hole in the stucco to test the wood. By this time, the corner was completely decayed and, as you've seen here, had to be rebuilt from the ground floor to the roof line.

corners and front porch. The realtor arranging the sale chose to ignore these additional problems, since the limited report is legally acceptable.

Sometimes the design of a home makes certain structural areas genuinely inaccessible to pest control inspection. The inspector should acknowledge this in the report and let the homeowner know whether inspection of these areas is worth the extra cost.

Missed infestations and conditions

Operators are responsible for identifying and, if so requested, for repairing all visible infestations and problem conditions in areas included in a report. Operators must often work in cramped, dark crawl spaces and attics in search of termites or mysterious sources of moisture. Occasionally, an operator may miss a subtle sign which, several months or even years later, makes itself obvious to the homeowner or another operator.

An operator's liability for missed infestations or conditions varies from state to state. In California, the Pest Control Board can compel an operator who has missed an infestation or condition to perform repairs and treatment at no additional charge to the homeowner. If the operator refuses, the company loses its license. In other states, a consumer may need to file a civil law suit to make the operator correct the situation.

In any case, justice comes most painlessly when consumers take quick action. To take advantage of California's relatively tough regulations, for example, homeowners need to bring complaints to the Structural Pest Control Board within two years after the operator at fault files a report or notice of completion. This statute of limitation is another reason (besides catching incipient infestations) why homes should be inspected every year and a half. For example, a couple bought a $145,000 house which had received a structural pest inspection, repair and treatment, and certification. After two and a half years, the couple decided to sell the house and asked the same operator to perform the necessary inspection. The operator found that the house needed $2,500 more work. It's highly unlikely, however, that this much new damage could have appeared in two and a half years. Most of this damage was missed when the company made the original inspection. If the couple had had their home reinspected a year earlier, they could have filed a complaint in time to meet the two-year deadline. The operator would have had to bear the cost of the missed infestation. Instead, the homeowners did.

Although the state board's deadline passed and the couple completed the repairs needed to sell the house, their case need not end here. They still have the option of bringing it to court and demanding compensation from the operator who missed the infestation. Of course, pursuing the matter in court is much more costly and risky than filing a complaint with the state board.

California's Structural Pest Control Board does not hold operators responsible for identifying hidden infestations or conditions, even if these problems become visible soon after the inspection. An infestation isn't missed unless it's visible. Operators don't need to probe beneath stucco siding, painted window sashes or other finished surfaces that show no signs of decay or water leaks, even when the design of the house makes these areas highly susceptible to damage. If you suspect that an unblemished surface in a house you want to keep or buy conceals damage, instruct the operator to probe it.

Unnecessary work

A homeowner loses money when repairs are made on the basis of an inaccurate inspection of an area that doesn't need repairs. Such a report may constitute fraud. Fortunately, this form of consumer fraud is relatively uncommon in the pest control industry. Pest control operators know that consumers can often spot an inaccurate description before repairs begin. They may know their home well or they may have ordered multiple reports. If an operator does give a homeowner a report that calls for work that turns out to be unnecessary, however, it can be difficult to prove that the operator's actions are fraudulent.

In such situations, the strength of the case against the operator depends on the report's clarity in identifying the infestation. A vaguely-written report with a price tag for extensive repair may look, to officials, more like overbidding than fraud. An unscrupulous operator with an eye out for high-profit repair work, for example, might find a small area of subterranean termite infestation, check the appropriate box on the report's list of possible problems and indicate on the diagram of the house the general location of the infestation without specifying where treatment and repair are needed. The operator might make a bid with repair of the larger area (including structurally solid areas) in mind. The homeowner might order a second report that indicates the infestation in specific detail and makes a bid for repair of the infested area alone. In comparison, the first report doesn't explicitly appear to prescribe more work than the second—it just appears to charge more for it. For this reason, operators should indicate the extent of termite and beetle infestation and decay as specifically as possible on their sketches of a house's substructure.

Another difficulty in proving fraud is the fact that it's often difficult for even the most competent operator to asses the full extent of pest damage until repair work begins and damaged wood is removed. Officials and operators recognize that the accuracy of diagrams on pest reports is always somewhat limited. In order to avoid becoming victims of fraud, then, homeowners need to use multiple reports and bids and the support of state licensing agencies who can hold the threat of disciplinary action against operators who write vague reports with high bids. In another case, a homeowner received an expensive repair bid from a pest control operator. To save money, the homeowner called another contractor (who wasn't a licensed pest control operator) to do the repairs. Once the contractor opened up sections of the house where the operator had indicated damage, the contractor found that most of the damage didn't really exist. The operator had reported too much. The homeowner saved himself quite a sum of money by calling in a second party to do the work—but he still had to bear the expense of repairing undamaged areas that the contractor, in good faith, had opened up to repair. This extra cost might have been saved if the homeowner had ordered reports from several operators before repair began.

Several legitimate repair practices can cost homeowners more than necessary. Operators often replace wooden elements such as windows, doors and eaves at high hourly rates. Homeowners could have repaired these items by themselves or by a carpenter at a lower cost.

Wood-frame windows, for example, tend to decay at the lower corners in climates that encourage condensation on the inside window panes. An inspector may recommend replacement of fungus-infected window sashes or even installation of new windows. The cost of each replacement can add up to an astronomical bid—it's not uncommon in the San Francisco area for a bid to call for $1,500 to $2,000 worth of wood sash. This price includes removing decayed sash, fitting in new sash which has been custom-made to size and painting the wood with primer, one finish color on the outside and another finish color on the inside.

If windows aren't too badly damaged, homeowners can repair them by "remanufacturing" (cutting away defective wood and splicing on sound wood) or by drilling out the punk wood, treating the affected area with a wood preservative and filling the holes with plastic wood or some other filler. Steel or brass reinforcement brackets can add strength to the repaired area, if necessary. Although sashes repaired this way aren't as pretty or sound as new windows, they can last as long as new windows and cost very little.

Homeowners can avoid another unnecessary addition to repair bids if they correct conditions of faulty grade, earth-wood contact, cellulose debris and excessive moisture themselves. Operators, obliged by state law to report faulty grade conditions, include labor and machinery charges for correcting this condition in their repair bids. These charges are usually unnecessarily high because the work is performed by an over-skilled worker who is already on the site (probably a carpenter).

Disagreement over recommended treatment

Whenever a homeowner requests pest control reports from several different operators, there's a good chance that the reports won't agree on the proper methods for correcting the pest problem, even if the reports do agree on the nature, extent and location of the infestation. If you find yourself in this case, you may face a difficult job of deciding whether one type of treatment is significantly better than another. Don't hesitate to ask the operators about the advantages and disadvantages of proposed treatments. Sometimes one treatment may be as good as another, but each reflects the differing experiences and preferences of the operators.

One frequent disagreement between pest control reports is whether or not to use a chemical treatment. In one case of a home with beetle damage, one operator recommended an expensive tenting and fumigation procedure. Another oper-

If windows are just slightly decayed, homeowners can save money be repairing the frames themselves. Punk wood should be removed and the holes filled. If the corners are decayed, they can be reinforced with brackets as shown here.

ator said that replacing the damaged wood would make fumigation unnecessary, although the home would need frequent inspection for reinfestation.

In a similar case, one operator recommended chemical pressure-treatment of a crawlspace to get rid of subterranean termites. Another operator thought it best to avoid chemicals entirely, since they are never a fool-proof guarantee against reinfestation. Instead, the operator wanted to break the termites' shelter tubes manually, reinspect the crawlspace every other year and break tubes as they reappeared.

Improper repairs or alterations

Repairing structural pest damage and correcting conditions that might lead to further infestation is an imperfect science at best. Homeowners should realize that operators don't always have control over the effectiveness of correctly performed work. However, if an operator uses a substandard or incorrect technique in a repair or alteration, the homeowner may justly hold the operator at fault.

Depending on the state, repairs and other changes in a home's structure may fall under the jurisdiction of the state pest control board or local building department. Some repairs require a building permit from the appropriate authority. When an operator takes out a building permit, the operator is held accountable for construction techniques.

Building codes were established to protect the public from unsafe construction practices (such as inadequate bracing for porches or steps) that could lead to injury. If an operator fails to apply for a building permit or fails to have completed work inspected, the operator may be liable for negligence.

State codes don't control the aesthetic quality of pest control work, so you need to check up on an operator's previous experience with decorative elements, such as stucco siding. You don't want to end up with stucco patterns as mis-matched as the two on this wall.

Poor workmanship or unfinished work

Official agencies can't intervene in disputes about the quality of workmanship in structural pest control repair unless the workmanship is so poor that it violates building codes. Work that passes inspection by the building department or the state structural pest control board may not satisfy you or be consistent with the quality of construction in your home. If quality workmanship means a lot to you, you might want to ask prospective operators for references—former customers that had similar repair work done (such as a new front porch, stucco repair or a foundation cap). Keep in mind that these references are no guarantee that work will always be of the same quality.

Discuss your concern for quality workmanship before repairs begin. Let the operator know that you want the best possible work from the repair crew. Operators aren't always able to recruit the most skilled craftsmen because pest control repair is often dirty, unpleasant work carried out in cramped spaces. Nonetheless, you have a right to expect the crew to perform at its best.

Cost constraints, the unavailability of special materials (such as wood mouldings) or the lack of skilled labor (to match a stucco pattern, for example) might make changes in architectural details necessary. If so, discuss these changes in advance. Make sure that you won't be disappointed halfway through repairs to learn that your chosen contractor's low bid was based on the use of materials other than what you expected (for example, replacement aluminum windows instead of custom-made, matching wood windows).

Improper use of pesticides

A pesticide is improperly used when it is stored, handled, applied or cleaned-up carelessly, when it is used ineffectively, or when it is banned completely or restricted from the use in question. Jurisdiction over an operator's use of pesticides usually rests with a state structural pest control board, a state agricultural board or a department of public health. The EPA regulates the manufacture and marketing of pesticides under the Federal Insecticide, Fungicide and Rodenticide Act of 1972. The EPA licenses pesticides and other hazardous chemicals for specific uses. As explained in Chapter 8, the use of many termiticides is restricted to subsurface ground insertion by certified applicators.

The arsenal of pesticides available to the pest control industry changes with time. As chemical companies develop new, less hazardous pesticides, they retire older ones from use. The EPA may initiate review of a pesticide's environmental impact that may ultimately lead to a ban. Operators need to keep abreast of these changes.

A pesticide must be applied so that it does its intended job but doesn't pose a health hazard to residents, pets or plants. Today, chemical companies examine pesticides' possible applications with an eye to maximizing effectiveness and minimizing health hazards, so that the most effective use of a pesticide is often the safest. Improper application may cause the pesticide to be ineffective and expose residents to an unwarranted risk. One chemical company that markets chlordane has received reports of improper application of their product by unlicensed do-it-yourselfers. In one case, a landlord tried to rid a rented home of subterranean termites by spraying chlordane in the basement. The tenant complained to the company about an odor that lingered and made her nauseous for weeks after the spraying. Even licensed operators make inexcusable mistakes—as did one New York exterminator who poured chlordane into a home's heating system at a rate 20 times higher than the federal safety level, forcing the couple that owned it to move into a tent and file a $20 million suit.

If a pesticide proves ineffective after its first application, the operator should find out why before trying again and risking further chemical exposure. Ineffective treatment may result from using the incorrect dilution, incorrect application technique or incorrect chemical. Usually, however, pesticide application problems arise because the chemical is handled or sprayed carelessly. The most common complaint from consumers who have had their homes treated with pesticide is about the unpleasant, lingering odor in living areas. This doesn't necessarily mean that the exterminator applied too much pesticide or applied it carelessly, as it did in the cases above. Instead, it often means that ventilation in these homes is inadequate and should be improved immediately.

You can best avoid complaints about pesticide treatment if you discuss the procedure with the operator before treatment begins. Follow the sug-

If these windows look a bit discordant to you, imagine how they must look to the homeowner whose custom-made wood window was replaced with an aluminum one. Read your operator's bid carefully, paying special attention to replacement materials. Some operators are able to make low bids by skimping on quality.

gestions in Chapter 8. If, despite these precautions, pesticide odor persists in your home or if occupants report symptoms of pesticide poisoning, call the operator back to get rid of the fumes. Most operators are very helpful in these situations because they occur frequently and can be solved with simple ventilation techniques.

If the odor lasts for weeks after treatment or the operator won't help you take care of the problem, you may want to contact local representatives of the state agency with jurisdiction over residential pesticide application. If you think that the fumes seriously jeopardize your family's health, call the local public health office for help. The office may send someone to help you judge the severity of the problem. In extreme cases, occupants may have to leave home until the contamination subsides.

Resolving consumer complaints

If something goes wrong during the process of structural pest inspection, repair or treatment, you'll need to find out which state agency is responsible for resolving your complaint. Appendix 2 is a directory of state agencies with jurisdiction over structural pest control. If the listed agency can't resolve your case, it can probably refer you to the one that can.

Once you understand your legal rights as a consumer, notify the pest control operator of what, specifically, you find unsatisfactory and what the operator needs to do to satisfy you. Try to be as businesslike as possible. Let the operator know that you would prefer to resolve the situation with the operator directly, although you are aware of the formal steps to take (such as filing a complaint or a lawsuit). Give the operator ample opportunity to see your side of the issue and to suggest a resolution. You may want to set a deadline for the operator to respond.

If you cannot get the operator to cooperate or if the operator has, in your judgement, immediately threatened the health and safety of your family through incompetence or negligence, file a complaint with the state pest control board, consumer protection agency or ombudsman. In California, consumers can file a complaint with the Pest Control Board for two dollars. The board will respond in 10 days. It may send an inspector to examine the situation and judge whether the operator is at fault. If so, the board can force the operator to correct the

problem by threatening to revoke the operator's license.

In some states, lack of such agencies may make it necessary to hire an attorney. If thousands of dollars or the health of your family are at stake, the attorney's fees may be worth the result of legal action. If the dispute involves a nominal sum, a suit in small claims court may be the easiest and least expensive way to resolve it.

Be aware that your state may have a deadline for filing pest control complaints. In California, it's two years. Homeowners have lost money by letting this deadline slip by. A major operator there once missed over $6,000 of work in a $72,000 home. Once the homeowner was made aware of this by a second contractor called in to do repairs, the homeowner could have held the first operator liable for the missed problems. However, the homeowner procrastinated, two years slipped by, and he eventually found he could no longer file a complaint. The value of the home has been hurt by rot left under the kitchen sink and considerable beetle damage.

In the final analysis, you will have to judge whether filing a formal complaint or pursuing legal action is worth your time and frustration. Structural pest control repair and treatment is dirty, messy work, and usually involves the use of dangerous chemicals. Both the consumer and the operator approach a job with incomplete information. If it is difficult for the operator to judge the full extent of the damage before repair begins, it is doubly difficult for the average consumer to anticipate what will happen to the home. Operators are usually well-paid for performing this unattractive job and yet, each year, many go bankrupt because of unanticipated problems.

Improving pest control regulations and practices

People have fought structural pests for thousands of years. In this country, we have gained some mastery over termites, beetles and fungi. The cost has been high, not only in terms of repair cost and inconvenience, but also in terms of exposure to dangerous chemical substances. Here is a list of practices that the pest control industry could develop or change in order to improve homeowners' security against structural pests.

1) Require inspections. In some areas of the United States, structural pest infestations are relatively rare because climate, construction practices or absence of pests make them unnecessary. In most states, however, structural pests are a serious problem. An infestation can spread through a house and cause thousands of dollars of damage before it's ever detected. The financial risks of buying an uninspected house are so high that it's difficult to understand why inspections aren't made a mandatory part of every real estate sale, especially in states like Florida, California and Hawaii. In these states, an agency for keeping reports on file already exists because the majority of homes are inspected at the time of sale anyway (partly as a result of mortgage lender requirements). These agencies could supervise the new inspection requirements.

2) Encourage more comprehensive inspection. An incomplete inspection can be more dangerous than no inspection at all, for it brings with it a false sense of security. A "termite inspection" is often an inspection of the substructure alone. Yet there are many other places where wood-destroying organisms can strike which are equally expensive to repair. We need a standardized vocabulary for specifying the location of infestations and for describing conditions that may lead to infestation, as well as an expanded inspection checklist of such conditions.

California's Structural Pest Control Act is a forerunner in the development of inspection guidelines, but since it was first written, experts have learned more about the conditions that encourage infestation. California's act, as well as those yet to be written in other states, would protect homeowners better if they included this knowledge. For example, experts now know that inset gutters on stucco homes often leak and cause the walls and corners of these houses to decay. Inspectors should be directed to check areas beneath inset gutters for decayed wood. If necessary, they should probe under finished surfaces, such as stucco siding and painted window sashes.

3) Develop a structural pest control code. Perhaps we need, as part of the uniform building code, a structural pest control code that would specify construction details for those areas prone to infestation. The code might, for example, prohibit inset gutters and require a 6-inch clearance between earth and wood for all structures, including fences and steps. This code would not only apply to new structures, but also to those undergoing repair or alteration.

4) Separate inspection from repair. In most of the United States, the same person (or company) determines whether structural pest damage is present, repairs the damage under contract and certifies that the home is free of infestation. This arrangement can produce a conflict-of-interest for the operator. Too many financial pressures influence reports as to the extent of structural damage. The more damage the inspector finds, the more profit the inspector's company is likely to make on the job. If the bid on the first report seems too high, a homeowner can order a second—but this seldom clarifies matters. The second report often identifies and makes a bid for repair of a different set of problems.

In addition, pest control operators can't always assess the full extent of structural damage until they begin tearing into walls and foundations. To protect themselves from unexpected problems, they make bids higher than needed to repair the expected damage. In short, the current arrangement undermines the reliability of pest control reports.

We need a system that eliminates inspectors' conflict-of-interest and gives operators and homeowners financial protection against concealed damage. First, the operator who inspects and certifies the house should be seperate from the operator who repairs the house. Second, inspectors need a way to guarantee inspections without making a high repair bid.

The system might be modeled after methods used to guarantee property titles. A homeowner would hire a pest control operator to perform a thorough inspection of the home. For a fee higher than the present cost, the operator would furnish a certified report specifying the necessary repairs. The operator would insure the accuracy of the report. The owner would then obtain competitive bids for the repairs outlined in the report from other contractors. If, after work began, the chosen contractor found additional structural pest damage, the contractor would repair that also and make a claim with the inspector's insurer for the additional repair cost. This system motivates the inspector to make a thorough, complete inspection. The repair contractor could then bid on the work in the same way as any other alteration job. Furthermore, the repair contractor would be motivated to do a thorough job since payment for repair of unexpected damage is guaranteed by the inspector's insurer.

The current owners of this home bought it as-is after reviewing a pest control report that they believed was complete. While remodeling the bathroom above the garage, they discovered rot under the floor. They removed the ceiling and walls of the garage and found that the whole side (above) was decayed. The wood was barely strong enough to support the floor above it. The culprit in this story, again, was an inset gutter (below). Water leaked behind the siding, leaving no signs to arouse a pest control inspector's suspicions. Considering all the cases of decay caused by inset gutters, perhaps inspectors should begin to regularly probe walls beneath them.

The missed infestation adds an unexpected $12,000 to the repair bill for this house. The decayed side will be entirely rebuilt. Until then, the house is held up by makeshift braces.

Chapter 10

How-To-Do-It: Repairing Damage in Your Home

When a real estate sale leads to the discovery of structural defects and pest damage, homeowners and buyers are often taken by surprise. What had seemed to be a sound home may need several thousand dollars worth of work. Sellers and buyers depend upon operators to provide an accurate picture of the home's condition and to restore its structural integrity. Yet inspection is no piece of cake, even for the most experienced operators. Reports may prove to be inaccurate and presumably complete repairs may leave significant infestations untouched, undermining the worth of the homeowner's most important investment.

Much of the distress caused by unfavorable reports—the snarls in real estate deals, pesticide contamination and dissatisfaction with operators' work—can be avoided when homeowners make inspection and repairs a regular responsibility. You might need the experience of a licensed pest control operator to name specific wood-destroying insects, detect infestations in hidden areas or apply pesticides, but you can often take care of the basics yourself. You can become aware of many of your home's defects just by living with them—especially drainage problems, leaks and excessively moist areas—and can easily recognize more when vulnerable areas are pointed out to you.

Selling your house—or simply living in it—will be easiest if you correct defects and infestations before a pest control inspection is made. Enlist the help of a carpenter or plumber if you need it— operators usually subcontract plumbing repairs anyway. Schedule repairs at your convenience, rather than rushing to meet a sale deadline. The do-it-yourself approach requires your time and concentration, but it saves money and brings your home closer to receiving a clean structural pest control report in the future.

Repairing some structural defects—such as a leaky roof or decayed walls with stucco siding— requires extensive carpentry skills and is best done by a specialist contractor. However, some of the most critical structural defects found in homes— faulty grades, leaking toilets and showers—can be repaired by homeowners with basic fix-up skills. This chapter shows you four techniques: capping a foundation, pouring a foundation curb, repairing a leaky shower and rebolting a toilet. The first is considered by some real estate agents and contractors to be a relatively complex project, so you may want to seek professional direction for your foundation cap. According to most building codes, all four jobs require a building permit and inspection. The second two also usually require a plumbing permit and inspection, though in practice handymen sometimes neglect this step.

Even if you don't have any fix-up skills whatsoever, you can still help maintain the structural integrity of your home. You might begin by removing debris and other articles made of wood, paper or cardboard from earth substructure floors, cleaning gutters or cutting back vines and bushes that keep siding moist. Chapter 5 gives you several suggestions of places to start.

Capping a foundation

If the top of your home's foundation is level with or below the ground outside, your house has a "faulty grade." The closer wood siding, mudsills and other substructural members come to contacting the earth, the easier it is for ground moisture to seep into the wood and encourage fungi to germinate. Subterranean termites have less work to do before their tubes reach wood. To keep wood safe, local building codes usually require that new foundations raise the mudsill six inches above the exterior grade.

If you're lucky, you can solve faulty grade and earth-wood contacts just by shoveling away earth and debris that have accumulated near the mudsill. In many cases, however, digging around at the base of a house can make matters worse by channeling rain water toward the walls or weakening an already shallow foundation. The best remedy for these homes may be to "cap" the foundation—shorten studs, rebuild the sill higher and pour concrete on top of the existing foundation. This procedure takes a bit of planning, some hard labor and some basic carpentry skills. By capping the foundation yourself, you might spend as little as an eighth of the cost of hiring an operator.

It's easiest to raise the foundation in four to eight-foot sections, even if you plan to raise the entire perimeter. Working in small sections allows you to avoid using jacks or building temporary supports. The house rests securely on its old foundation while you work underneath.

Check the studs in the section you've chosen to cap. If they're at least 90 percent free of termite damage and completely free of decay, leave them in. Check the exterior siding. If it's made of good stucco or wood, you may want to leave it intact so it can serve as the exterior formboard for the concrete pour, even though it forces you to work under the house. If the siding isn't worth saving, remove it and work from the outside. Mark a line across the good studs six to eight inches above the exterior grade with a chalked string. Cut off the bottom of the studs along the line with a chainsaw, a reciprocating saw (such as a Sawzall) or a circular saw with a worm drive (such as a Skilsaw). Remove the old mudsill.

If the existing studs, plates or sheathing show any signs of infestation or decay, replace them. Cut the new studs so the bottoms are even at the proper grade.

Choose a pressure-treated mudsill—or, if you want to avoid chemicals, one made of redwood. Cut

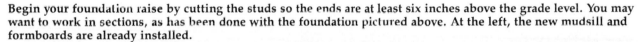

Begin your foundation raise by cutting the studs so the ends are at least six inches above the grade level. You may want to work in sections, as has been done with the foundation pictured above. At the left, the new mudsill and formboards are already installed.

Some homes have exterior siding, like stucco, that is strong enough to serve as a form for the concrete pour. Leave this siding intact (1) and cut the studs (2) from the inside. Remove wood sheathing so siding is exposed up to the bottom of the studs (3). Hold the mudsill up to the studs and mark it where you will drill holes for all-thread bars (4). Make sure that there are vents in the siding through which you can pour concrete over the old foundation (5).

Plan for the skeleton of your foundation cap to look something like this. All-thread bars (1) should be placed between studs and near the end of each length of mudsill. The ends of the bars should extend three inches into the foundation (six to 10 in earthquake-prone areas) (2). When the nuts around the all-thread bars are tightened, the sill will be held firmly against the bottom of the studs. Rebar should be fastened to the bars with tie wire (3). If you've kept the exterior siding intact and plan to pour concrete from outside, each section should have a vent next to a gap in the mudsill (4). The bottom of the vent should be no lower than the mudsill.

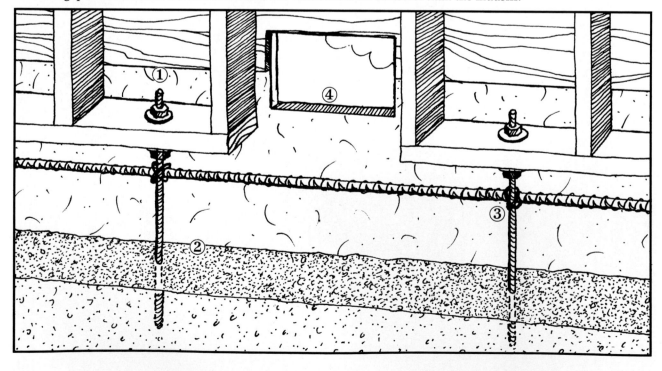

it to the length of the section you will raise. You might also want to attach termite-proofing sheet metal to the bottom of the sill at this point.

The new mudsill will be held against the bottom of the studs by all-thread bars. These bars also bolt the mudsill to the foundation. The bottom end of each bar is inserted into a hole in the foundation, and the top end into a hole in the mudsill. Plan to drill holes for approximately three bars in each eight-foot section. The bars should be two to four feet apart in areas prone to earthquakes and six feet apart elsewhere. One bar should be placed at each end of a section of mudsill and at least one bar should support the middle. It's better to use too many bars than too few, since extra bars won't add much to the cost of the foundation and will also work like housejacks during the raise.

Use 1/2-inch all-thread bars for a one-story house and 5/8-inch bars for a two story house in most areas. Use 3/4-inch bars for a two-story dwelling in earthquake-prone areas. Cut the bars long enough to extend from the top of the new mudsill to a depth of three inches into the old foundation (or six to 10 inches in earthquake-prone areas).

Once you've planned the placement and size of the bars, drill the holes in the mudsill and founda-tion. All-thread bars must be installed plumb. To make sure each pair of holes is perfectly aligned, set the mudsill directly on the section of foundation you will raise. At the proper places, drill through the mudsill and foundation in one straight line. Set the sill aside and make sure the holes in the foundation are the proper depth. Drill them a little larger in diameter than the bars you plan to use. Clean debris out of the holes.

With nuts and washers holding the all-thread bars to the mudsill, lift the sill to the studs and place the ends of the bars in the foundation. Pour an epoxy cement into the holes. Tighten the nuts and washers around the bars—first the pair beneath the sill, then the pair above it—so the sill is pushed up against the studs.

If your house needs releveling, this is a good time to do it. Back nuts and washers away from the sill along the sides that need lifting. Tighten the bottom nuts with a long-handled wrench so that the sill is pushed up 1/8 to 1/4 inch (or extend house-jacks, if you're using them). You'll need assistants to tighten each nut in the section at the same time. You may also need to score the siding if it is attached to anything below the mudsill. Check the house with a water level, and continue to lift if necessary. Be-

The holes for each all-thread bar in mudsill and foundation need to line up perfectly straight. Place the mudsill on the section of foundation to be capped. At the proper intervals, drill through the mudsill and through the founda-tion, so that each pair of holes is drilled at once in a straight line. The holes in the foundation should then be made slightly larger than the all-thread bars you plan to use.

After you drill and clean out the holes in the foundation, attach the all-thread bars loosely to the mudsill with nuts and washers. Place the mudsill into position over the foundation and insert the bars.

ware—once the base of the house is level, you might find that doors and windows look askew and need to be reset.

Once the bars are tightly in place, fasten rebar to them with tie wire. If you're doing this in sections, you should cut the rebar so it will overlap adjoining sections one foot to 18 inches.

Build formboards for the concrete pour with 1-by-12 inch No. 3 pine. Drill pairs of small holes just below the middle of each board. Plan for each pair to fall opposite an all-thread bar when the board is placed flush against the bottom of the existing foundation. Thread a wire through each pair of holes, looping it once around the bar. Leave the loose ends sticking out of the holes.

Foundations are usually wider than mudsills. When a formboard stands against the existing foundation, there should be a gap of about three inches between the top of the board and the sill. You'll soon pour concrete through this space. Join formboards to the mudsill with spacers cut from scrap wood. Screw one end of each spacer to a formboard and the other to the sill so your hand can slip into the gap and the formboard is straight. This space also makes it easier to wrap wire between boards and bars. Tightly twist the ends of the wires sticking out of the holes below so the board is held firmly in place.

Once the mudsill assembly is in position, pour epoxy cement into the holes in the foundation, around the ends of the all-thread bars. This binds the bars to the old foundation.

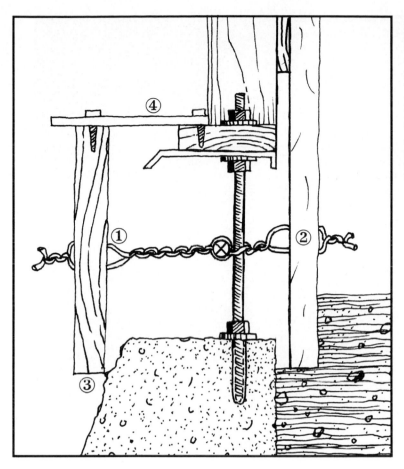

Hold formboards in place by fastening to all-thread bars with tie wire. There should be a pair of small holes near the middle of each formboard so wire can be wrapped from board to bar (1). If the exterior siding is weak or if you are installing a formboard in place of siding, you should also secure it with wire (2). Twist the ends of the wire so the bottom edge of the formboard is tight against the foundation (3). The foundation is usually wider than the mudsill, so you may need to install spacers to keep the form-board upright (4).

From the substructure, the foundation should look like this when you're ready to pour concrete through the vent (1). Look behind the formboard (2) to make sure that the wires that hold the formboards are secure. Clean debris from the old foundation (3).

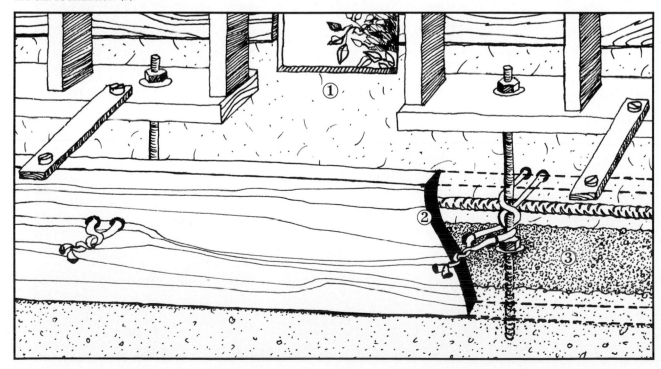

This corner section is almost ready for the concrete pour. The formboards, lying on the substructure floor, just need to be tied into place.

Sometimes a foundation needs to be raised so high that you need to build extra-wide formboards. This formboard is made of two long boards nailed to a shorter one. This carpenter twists the tie wires so the board will be tight against the foundation. You may also use ¾ CDX plywood, cut to the proper height, as a formboard.

If there are gaps between the substructure floor and the bottom of the formboards, fill them in with dirt to keep concrete from oozing out. If you're capping the foundation in sections, dam the open end (or both ends, if it's the first section) with a narrow formboard.

At last, you're ready to pour the concrete. Contact a company that rents concrete pumps (the usual cost is about $150 for three hours). From a ready-mix concrete supplier, order "six-sack pea gravel pump mix" concrete (this means that there are six sacks of cement mixed with pea-sized gravel in a cubic yard of concrete). Coordinate the delivery of the mix with the arrival of the concrete pump truck.

Concrete is ordered by the cubic yard. Usually, six or seven cubic yards are enough for the entire foundation. Measure the section you're capping before placing your order. It's better to make a high estimate than a low one. You can always use the extra concrete to reinforce the center of the house with concrete piers or to rat-proof the front porch with a concrete substructure floor.

Pump the mixed concrete through the vents, tap the forms with a hammer to make sure the concrete has settled into every space and let the new foundation cure for a couple of days. Remove the formboards and raise wood siding to the proper grade level. Hand-pack mortar into any gaps left between the foundation and new sill and let it harden. Finally, reinforce the connection between studs and sill by toe-nailing with two 16-penny nails on each side of the stud.

Now you may sit back and savor your hard-earned security from subterranean termites and fungi, or just rest up for work on the next section of the foundation.

A gap is left in this mudsill for the concrete pour. Notice how the formboard is held in place by tie wire.

The top edge of this formboard is held at an even distance from the mudsill by spacers made of scrap wood. Spacers help keep formboards from tilting under the pressure of wet concrete.

Brick foundations tend to be weak, and it's a good idea to cap them whether or not they're below grade. The first steps for capping a brick foundation are the same as for a concrete foundation: cut the studs to the proper level and drill holes for all-thread bar in the mudsill. However, since brick crumbles easily, don't drill holes for the bars in the foundation. Instead, the bars stand on the top of the foundation with nuts and washers at the bottom ends to serve as footings. The sill-and-bar assembly is held in place by the pressure of the sill against the bottom of the studs. Tie rebar to the bars with wire.

Brick foundations need a saddle cap for extra reinforcement. A saddle cap envelopes the brick in concrete. To build the frame for a saddle cap, dig a trench one foot deep and three inches wide on either side of the brick foundation. Bend rebar into the shape of a horseshoe—this is called a saddle tie. Hang saddle ties from the straight rebar in between the all-thread bars, and fasten them with tie wire. The ends of the saddle ties should dangle over the trenches. Tie the ends to straight lengths of rebar on each side of the foundation. Place formboards at the edge of the trench. Instead of fastening them to all-thread bars with wire, brace the boards from the outside with stakes.

Pour the concrete from the exterior side of the foundation. When the concrete has settled, taper the exterior top away from the mudsill for drainage. Remove the formboards.

To cap a brick foundation, left, a new mudsill is held against the cut studs by all-thread bars. The brick foundation is surrounded by a rebar frame that will reinforce the new foundation. Concrete will be poured around the structure to the height of the mudsill.

A capped brick foundation may not be strong enough to withstand the forces that homes in areas prone to earthquakes may face. The brick foundation of this home is being replaced entirely with a stronger concrete foundation. The home stands on concrete piers until the job is completed.

Pouring a foundation curb

Sometimes, a house with faulty grade has structural problems that make it impossible to lower the surrounding ground level or cap the foundation. If you find yourself in this predicament, don't despair—you can still pour a concrete curb beside the foundation. Curbs give wood in the substructure a few extra inches of protection.

It's almost always better to pour an entire curb at once. If the top of the existing foundation is below grade, dig a ditch three inches wide and deep enough to expose the top of the foundation. Mark the exterior walls with a chalk line six to eight inches above grade (the grade is the ground level as far as four feet from the house, not the bottom of the ditch). If the siding is stucco, score it deep along the line with a masonry blade attached to a circular saw. If the siding is wood, attach a wood blade—but choose an inexpensive one since it could be ruined if it hits nails in the siding. Knock out the siding below the line with a hammer. Remove the exposed sheathing to the same level that you removed the siding.

Inspect the wood substructural members that you have just exposed for termites and fungus growth. You may need to replace the mudsill, floor and rim joists before constructing the curb.

Roll out a sheet of metal flashing (such as rolled sheet metal) that is wide enough to cover all the wood from the foundation to the sheathing. Place the top edge under the sheathing. Nail the flashing to the studs along a straight line and leave the nails sticking out one-half inch. Set rebar on the nails and tie it to them with wire.

Build formboards out of 2-by-6 inch douglas fir, standard grade or better. Prop the formboards by nailing them at the bottom to the end of a 2-by-4. Place another board at a 45 degree angle between the formboard and the 2-by-4. Place the formboard upright three inches away from the wall (or at the edge of the ditch) and drive a stake in at the other end of the 2-by-4. This will keep the formboard from moving back when concrete is poured.

You can use a lower grade of concrete mixture for the curb than for a foundation (five-sack instead of six-sack pea gravel pump mix) because the curb doesn't support the house. Pour it so that the curb is three to four inches above the grade. The top of the curb should be level. Once it dries, fill in the space between the curb and the bottom of the sheathing with stucco. Slope the stucco to the outer edge of the curb. After you remove the formboards, you might also want to put stucco over the front of the curb—an easy way to give the curb a cosmetic touch-up.

To pour a curb, dig the earth away from the top of the foundation (1). Remove siding and sheathing so the bottom edges (2) are six to eight inches above grade level.

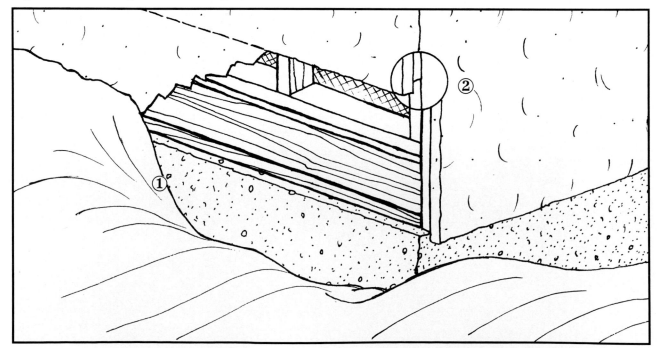

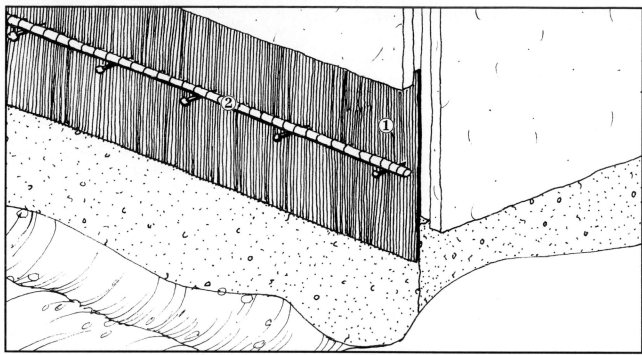

Cover the exposed area, from the top of the foundation to the bottom edge of the sheathing, with a sheet of metal flashing (1). Attach the flashing to the studs with a row of nails. Lay rebar on the nails (2) and fasten it with tie wire.

Prop up formboards (1) three inches away from the side of the house with a 2-by-4 and a stake (2). If necessary, dig the ditch around the foundation a little more so it's even with the formboard. Pour concrete into this space until it's three to four inches above grade (3). Let the concrete dry, then fill in the angle between the sheathing and concrete with stucco (4).

Repairing a leaky shower

A leaking shower stall provides fungi in the bathroom and substructure with a constant source of moisture. An apparently functional shower may stand on a subfloor so decayed that it could send a bather plummeting to the depths of the basement at any moment. The leak may increase humidity in the substructure so that moisture builds up in all areas—not just those adjacent to the shower.

If an inspection of your shower reveals leaks in the shower pan, the tile, or the flanges that trim plumbing valves, you might want to consider replacing the shower stall yourself. The carpentry skills necessary for this job depend upon the extent of the damage. You might need to replace a good portion of the bathroom floor, or you might only need to replace tile and fittings—a creative task that allows you to change the look of your bathroom.

If water has leaked into the wood behind and underneath the stall, you'll need to remove the fittings, tile and shower lining. Fix any floor joists that have begun to decay. Rebuild the subfloor (to insure yourself against future leaks, use pressure-treated wood), walls and the dam that forms the perimeter of the shower pan. You may also need to install a new drain with flanges that don't leak.

Install narrow lengths of waterproof sheetrock over the stall floor alongside the base of the dam. Next to that, build a smooth slope down to the middle of the stall floor with Fix-all.

Line the stall floor with a vinyl pan. You'll need to fold the pan to fit the shower yourself. Make a pattern of the inner stall floor and mark its edges on the vinyl. Leave enough vinyl beyond the floor line so that the sides of the pan, when folded up along the line, extend at least three inches above the shower dam. Place the pan onto the stall floor and smooth out wrinkles, working out from the drain. When you reach a wall, fasten the top edge of the side to the studs. When you reach the dam, fold the corners so the excess vinyl is outside the pan, against the dam. Turn the sides of the pan over the dam. Tack the pan sides with nails placed at least two inches above the outside base of the dam. Cut an opening in the pan for the drain and seal the lining to it with a clamping ring.

Install 4-by-8 pieces of waterproof sheetrock over the wall studs so that the factory edge is at the bottom and is at least one inch above the height of the dam. The bottom of the sheetrock may overlap the lining. While installing the sheetrock, cover the vinyl pan with cardboard to keep it from being punctured.

Before you install a new shower pan, you may need to rebuild the floor underneath. This corner shower has a new floor and dam. The dam serves as the frame for the sides of the shower pan.

Form the slope of the shower floor by applying Fix-all from the dam down to the drain, as shown here.

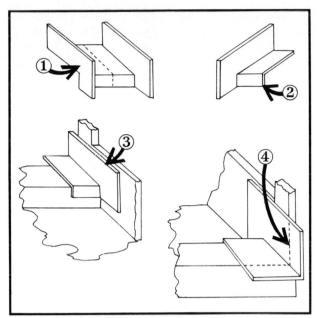

After you've installed the vinyl shower pan, attach dam corners. These plastic gadgets reinforce the corners between the walls and dam. They come in pairs that you separate down the middle (1). Place each half on the dam so that the apron (2) falls over the inside of the pan and the vertical side (3) is flush against a wall. Part of the dam corner will stick outside of the dam. Cut the flaps apart to the outer edge of the dam (4). Cement the dam corners in place with the flaps folded back to the dam and wall.

Reinforce the corners between the walls and dam—areas that are particularly likely to leak—by cementing dam corners over the pan. The dam corners come in pairs that you separate down the middle. Place each dam corner so the apron falls over the inside of the pan and the long, vertical side is flush against the wall. Cut the outer dam corner until the cut reaches the outer edge of the dam. Remove the dam corner and apply cement to its bottom and to the dam and wall. Replace the dam corner and fold the outer edges flush against dam and wall.

Smooth mortar over the pan, up along the walls to the sheetrock, and over the dam to the outer bottom edge. Once the mortar is dry, spread a surface of mastic over it. Lay the tile over the mastic. Tile comes in an array of colors from solid pastel shades to bright, hand-painted designs, so you can have a little fun planning the look of the new shower.

Finish the job with new plumbing fixtures—faucet, shower head, hot and cold water valves. This task also gives you a great deal of creative license.

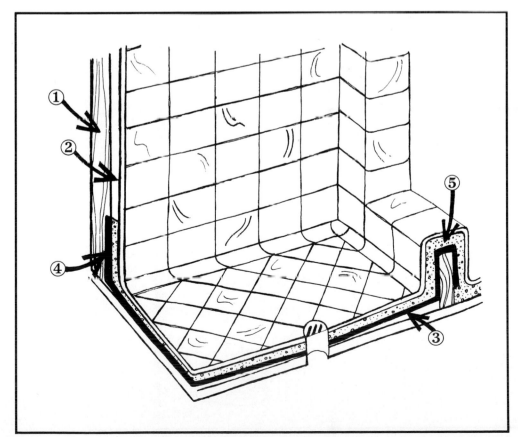

A finished shower is made of several layers of material that help keep water from reaching the wood subfloor and walls (1). From one inch above the height of the dam, walls are covered by waterproof sheetrock (2). The floor is covered by a slope of Fix-all (3). Over the Fix-all and dam lies the vinyl shower pan (4). Mortar covers the side of the wall up to the bottom edge of the sheetrock, the pan and dam (5). Tile—the only layer most homeowners ever see—forms the surface.

Rebolting a toilet

Like a leaky shower stall, a leaky toilet may encourage fungus growth in the floor underneath and excessive moisture conditions in the substructure. The toilet, however, usually doesn't need to be replaced (of course, if you have your eye on a chic new water closet, this is the time to install it). The leak could be due to failure of the wax seal between the toilet outlet and drain, the flange around the drain or the drain bend itself. As you remove and rebolt the toilet, inspect each of these connections for holes and signs of corrosion. If the bend and flange are solid and fit tightly together, you don't need to replace them.

Begin by turning off the water supply to the toilet. Flush the toilet until you've drained out all the water you can. Bail out the water that remains in the tank behind the seat with a cup. If you can't remove all of the water, prepare yourself and your bathroom for a bit of a mess.

Place a bucket under the water valve leading to the toilet to catch drips of water while you loosen that connection. Unbolt the toilet at its base. This is usually a very simple operation. Unscrew the nut and washer on either side of the base. Lift the toilet up and set it down on its side. Occasionally, the bolts are so tightly wedged into the base that you have to cut off the tops of the bolts with a hacksaw blade first. Check the area around the drain in the

Before you disconnect your toilet, turn the water valve off and flush water out. Place a bucket under the valve to catch dripping water when you unscrew the valve connection (1). Unbolt the toilet and lift it off the flange (2). Sticking out from under the toilet, you'll see a plastic cylinder (3) surrounded by a wax seal (4) that's probably faulty.

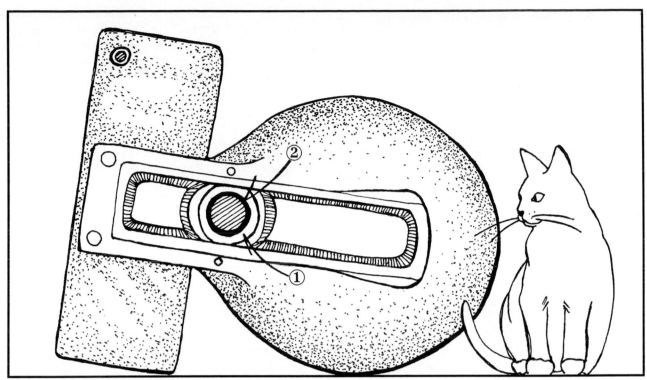

Set the toilet on its side while you make repairs. Remove the wax seal (1) and plastic cylinder (2) and install a new pair. When you replace the toilet, make sure the plastic cylinder goes down straight into the drain. An alternative method is to install the new wax seal and plastic cylinder in the drain instead of the toilet base, then carefully set the toilet down over the wax seal.

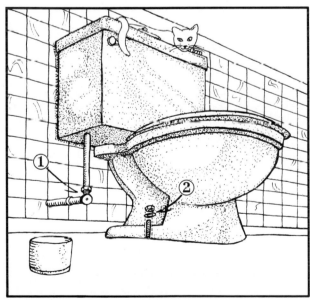

Screw nuts and washers over the new bolts (1) and reconnect the water valve (2).

floor for decay. Replace damaged wood in the subfloor and joists. Replace the flange if it is loose or corroded and screw the new flange to the floor with brass or galvanized screws. If the bend is corroded or made of lead, you should replace it with a cast iron or plastic (ABS) bend and install the appropriate flange.

With the toilet on its side, remove the wax seal that rings the outside of the toilet outlet. Install a new wax seal. If the weather is cold, the wax seal may be too stiff to stick properly. Warm it to 70 or 80 degrees.

Slide new bolts into the slots in the flange so they line up with the holes in the toilet base. Lift the toilet and insert the outlet into the drain as evenly as possible. The new wax ring should seal tightly against the inside of the drain as the base slides over the bolts. Screw washers and nuts onto the bolts, but not so tightly that the porcelain base cracks. Reconnect the water valve.

Turn the water back on and flush the toilet once. Make sure no water leaks over the floor or substructure. If it does, the flange may be improperly fitted and you'll have to remove the toilet and fix it again.

A warning about decks

You've learned techniques for correcting structural damage in foundations and bathrooms. Of the problems that can be corrected by a non-specialist handyman within the main structure of a house, these are the most critical.

Certain additions to the central structure also demand the attention of pest-conscious home-owners—decks, in particular. An improperly-built deck can become a breeding ground for fungi and can introduce infections to the house. The most common decay-encouraging problem is the lack of space between deck planks. Debris, such as leaves,

To make sure that a newly-built deck won't fall prey to fungus infections before its time, follow these few simple construction tips. Set all posts and bottom steps on concrete footings (1), in accordance with building codes. Bend metal flashing around the top and sides of all stair treads (2) and joists (3), as is demonstrated on one pair below. Leave enough space between deck planks so that debris and water can fall easily between them (4).

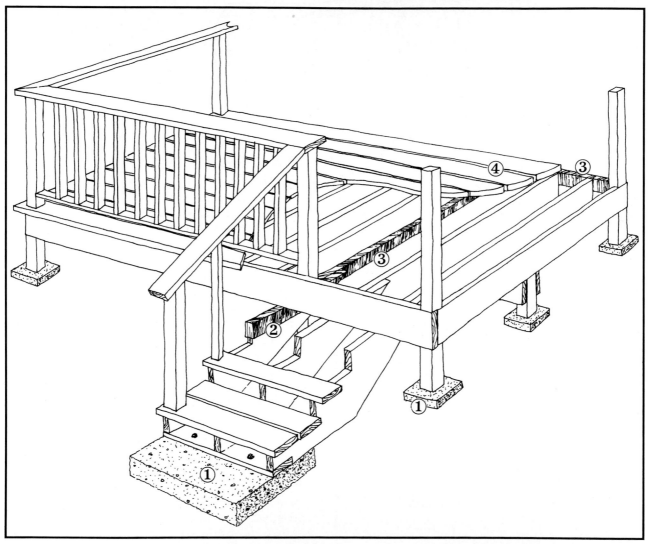

falls into the cracks between the planks, becomes trapped, and collects water from rain and other sources. The moist debris encourages fungus infections in joists and planks.

Once decks rot, they can be expensive and time-consuming to repair. It's important to take preventive measures against decay when you're having a deck remodeled or added to the house. These measures include designing the deck so that posts and stairs rest on concrete piers rather than on the earth. The joists and stair treads that support the deck planks should be waterproofed with metal flashing that is folded over the top and sides of the joists. When joists are flashed, water will run down the sides. Planks should be spaced far enough apart that debris can fall freely between them to the ground. These details of decay-preventive design may add 5 percent to the cost of the deck, but it may double or triple the deck's life.

This deck is relatively new, but its planking and joists have already begun to rot. Its decay has been hastened by the moisture-retaining dirt and leaves that you see trapped between the tightly-spaced planks.

Chapter 11

Structural Safety in Earthquake Zones

The purpose of home maintenance should go beyond minimizing the work and expense that might be demanded when a home is sold. The ultimate concern of any structural maintenance program is the strength and longevity of a home. These qualities of structural integrity lie in the wood framework behind a home's visible features.

One of the most serious tests of the structural integrity of a home is an earthquake. In many ways, the immediate impact of an earthquake should be of greater concern to homebuyers than the slower effects of termites, rot and beetles. Earthquakes bring devastation suddenly, and homeowners should be prepared.

During an earthquake, the ground shakes up and down and back and forth. The bulk of a house resists this movement, but buried footings or foundations shift with the ground. The opposing forces of inertia and the quake put considerable stress on the structural members between the roof and foundation. The walls and their connections to roof and foundation need to be strong enough to resist these forces, or else the house will rip apart. The house could fall off its foundation or the roof could slide off the walls. A homeowner's potential for loss in an earthquake is immense. In the worst cases, houses are rendered totally uninhabitable.

Many American homes will never face such a test. However, in areas prone to earthquakes, homes stand a tremendous risk of being reduced to rubble if structural defects and infestation aren't repaired. A 5.9 earthquake in Whittier, California in 1987 caused 22 million dollars in damage. Many homes were condemned immediately. Older buildings with structural weaknesses were hit hardest.

A 5.9 earthquake split this column on a porch in Whittier, California. The column had been weakened by rot that was hidden under the masonry exterior.

110

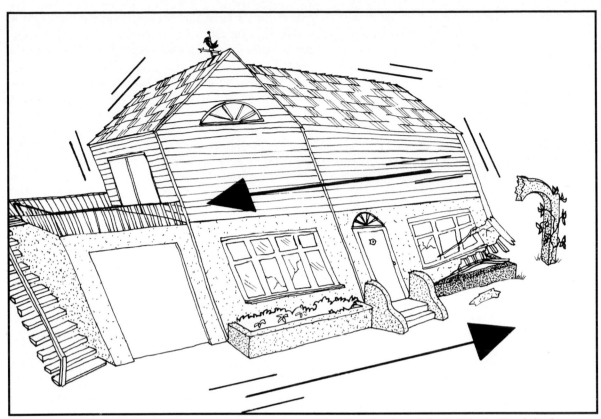

During an earthquake (top), the ground shakes a house's footings back and forth. The bulk of the house doesn't move quite as fast and resists the shaking movement. The opposition between the movements of the house and the ground strain the wood elements that carry the weight of the house. The more decayed these wood elements are, the more likely it is that the opposing forces in an earthquake will tear the house apart (bottom).

Stucco, brick and stone walls often give the illusion of solidity; the wood framework underneath these surfaces, however, is highly vulnerable to decay. Water from roof leaks, plumbing leaks and other sources is trapped inside the walls by the siding. Inset gutters are especially likely to allow water to leak between the siding and the wood frame. As soon as trapped moisture encourages fungus growth, the wood may lose as much as 80 percent of its strength. These conditions, if allowed to continue, may cause the home to lose much of its structural integrity.

If you live in earthquake country, you can't afford to be taken in by cosmetic solidity. You should be willing to have inaccessible areas opened and finished surfaces carefully probed for infestation and decay, especially if you have an older home. When problem conditions and pest damage are repaired, you should also consider reinforcing your home with structural elements known as "seismic retrofits." Retrofits bring homes in earthquake-prone areas a few valuable steps closer to structural security.

Homeowners should evaluate the risks of seismic damage against the expense of seismic reinforcements. It is easy to become complacent, since earthquakes occur randomly and infrequently even in geologically unstable regions (there is often a gap of a century between major earthquakes). It is possible, however, to estimate a home's potential for earthquake damage by considering the individual site, orientation and size of the home. Hillside homes and those built on unstable soil formations should be given extra attention. A standard foundation reinforcement may be adequate for a one-story home on a flat site, but a multi-story home on a hilly site may demand more extensive support to resist the strong lateral forces of a tremor.

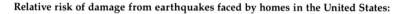

Relative risk of damage from earthquakes faced by homes in the United States:

No damage	0
Minor damage	1
Moderate damage	2
Major damage	3

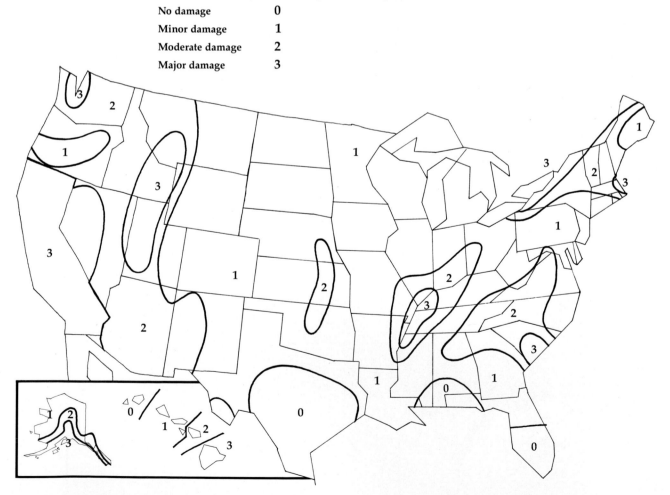

The finished surfaces of a home may hide the slow spread of a fungus infestation. If decay fungi take hold of structural members that support the weight of the house—such as joists, studs and sills—the house loses a great deal of strength. The major controllable cause of decay in homes is leaking water. Inset gutters, like those on this house, tend to leak and encourage decay in corners.

Inset gutters can cause decay in the parts of a home that are most critical to resisting earthquake forces. Inset gutters are built into the walls. You can see the ends of gutters that protrude through the exterior walls and end in gutter leaders in the photos at left and below. When inset gutters leak, water enters the wood within the walls rather than running down the exterior siding. Dark stains under the gutters in the photos on the left-hand page indicate that the walls beneath the siding are probably decayed.

This diagram shows that structural features that can make an inset gutter so dangerous to the strength of a wall. The gutter (1)—whether made of wood, aluminum or copper—is attached to an inch-thick board (2) that is nailed to the ends of the roof rafters (3). When the rafters extend no farther than the plate (4) and wall studs (5), the gutter is "inset" behind the siding material (6) of wood, stucco or brick. When the gutter leaks, the adjacent board, rafter ends, plates and studs become wet. With the help of warm air in the house that rises toward the roof, fungi infect these consistently wet areas. Though leaky inset gutters cause extensive decay in structurally critical areas, inspectors often fail to check them and building codes contain no restrictions against them. The problems of inset gutters could be completely avoided if the gutters were attached to rafters that extended beyond the walls. Then, if the gutters ever leaked, water would drip harmlessly to the ground.

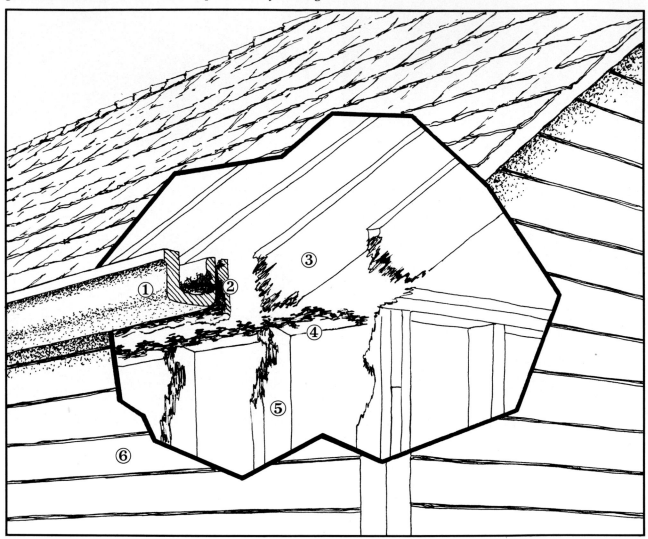

The inset gutter along the roofline of the stucco house above allowed water to leak into the corners. By the time that the stucco siding was removed during a remodeling job (above right), fungi had eaten away the wood corners from roofline to foundation. The mudsill (right) was almost hollow. Had an earthquake struck before the walls were repaired, the house would surely have crumbled.

The house in Whittier pictured above left was condemned after the 1987 earthquake—a tragedy due, in
part, to decay and improper reinforcement. The house
had rested on an old foundation with a decayed mudsill. The lateral forces of the earthquake encountered
no resistance at this connection and the house slid off
the foundation, three feet to the left (left). The stud
wall collapsed under the house's weight, the sheathing ripped off and the building crashed to the ground
(above). The corners split apart (right). Inside, the
floors buckled, walls collapsed, and windows shat-
tered. This near-total destruction of a 4-unit house
worth about $250,000 could probably have been
averted had the owner invested $15,000 in a reinforced
stud wall, a new foundation and repairs to structural
pest damage.

Seismic retrofits

It would probably be to everyone's advantage if building codes required seismic retrofits whenever a significant amount of repairs were done on a home in earthquake-prone areas. Retrofitting a shear wall after a foundation cap, for example, adds just 10 to 20 percent to the cost of the structural repair. When repairs are performed as part of a real estate transaction, buyer and seller can share the expense of these retrofits. Currently, however, earthquake risks are seldom given any thought by buyers, sellers, pest control operators or building departments. Protection from earthquake damage depends on you.

This chapter describes some of the most important seismic retrofits—anchor bolts, shear walls, plywood blocking and metal connectors. Though it's easiest to retrofit a house when structural members are exposed during repairs or renovations, the first two retrofits can be added to a good foundation that is intact. If your foundation is not in good shape—if it is constructed of substandard concrete (concrete foundations in older homes may have weakened with time) or if it is made of bricks—you may need to cap the foundation as discussed in Chapter 10 or replace it entirely.

Brick foundations: a special problem

Many people advocate the capping or saddling of old brick foundations, but this author believes that method to be extremely inadequate in most cases. A brick foundation usually consists of two or three rows of brick which are held together with mortar alone. Over time, the mortar breaks down and the foundation is weakened. There are often no metal reinforcements of any kind. A cap—which consists of four inches of concrete over the top and sides of the brick, attached with metal rebar—adds strength and bulk to the foundation. A cap may be fine in areas without earthquakes. Yet, this method of reinforcement provides none of the additional footing that is necessary to resist the lateral movement of a strong tremor. The shaking of an earthquake will further weaken the brick and mortar, leaving a concrete shell that lacks interior strength. This shell cannot adequately support the structure.

If your home has a brick foundation, the only way to feel confident of its strength is to replace it entirely. Capping or saddling old bricks isn't worth the expense and effort when it doesn't guarantee

peace of mind. The money is more wisely spent on replacing the foundation. Often, the cost of a replacement is only slightly higher than the cost of capping or saddling.

Retrofitting anchor bolts

Many homes built before World War II have mudsills that aren't anchored firmly enough to foundations to resist the force of an earthquake. If you've capped your foundation according to the suggestions for earthquake-prone areas in Chapter 10, the mudsill is now anchored with all-thread bars as securely as is practical. If you have a good concrete foundation to begin with, installing anchor bolts is a simple way to improve that connection.

You'll need anchor bolts that have a collar at one end that expands when the bolt is installed in the foundation. These are also known as expansion bolts or drop-in bolts, and are sold under the brand names Quik Bolt, Redhead, Stud, Wej-it and Parabolt. Use seven-inch long, $\frac{1}{2}$-inch bolts to anchor a small, one-story house. Use $8\frac{1}{2}$-inch long, $\frac{5}{8}$-inch bolts for two-story and large one-story houses. Use ten-inch long, $\frac{3}{4}$-inch bolts for three-story houses.

Drill holes for the bolts down through the mudsill and foundation with a rotary hammer. Attach masonry bits the same diameter as the bolt you will use, and set the rotary hammer's depth gauge to the depth required by the bolt. Drill the holes no more than four feet apart and place one at each end of a section of mudsill.

A handful of older homes have foundations reinforced with rebar. You'll know whether yours is one of them if the drill bit binds several times at a depth of three or four inches—that's when it will hit rebar. Position the new holes half an inch away from the rebar and an inch to the side of the misdrilled holes. Most new foundations also have rebar, but this problem rarely arises since they seldom require retrofit anchor bolts.

Occasionally, the space between mudsill and subfloor is too tight—less than two feet—to allow a rotary hammer to drill the holes vertically. Instead, you can bolt a metal plate to the side of the foundation and sill. The plate should be of $\frac{1}{8}$-inch thick steel and wide enough to extend from the top of the mudsill to at least five inches below the top of the foundation. Predrill holes along the top edge of the plate (which will be placed against the sill) for $\frac{1}{2}$-inch lag bolts and along the bottom edge for $\frac{1}{2}$-inch anchor bolts. Find lag bolts half as long as the width of the sill and anchor bolts half as long as the width of the foundation. Hold the drilled plate against the sill and foundation, mark the position of the holes with chalk and set the plate aside. Drill the holes in sill and foundation horizontally and replace the plate.

Whether drilling a hole vertically or horizontally, always blow it clean of concrete dust with a narrow plastic tube. Double-check the depth of the hole. When that's done, put a washer and a nut on the bolt. Pound the bolt into the hole with a sledgehammer until the only things that stick out are the washer on the sill, the nut and half of the threads. Tighten the nut firmly with a wrench. Inside the foundation, the collar will expand to enlarge the bottom of the anchor bolt by one-eighth inch. An earthquake would have to exert several tons of pressure on the house to pull out just one anchor bolt. Together, a row of bolts makes the sill and foundation almost inseparable.

Anchor bolts reinforce the connection between a solid mudsill and a concrete foundation so that it can withstand the tons of pressure exerted by an earthquake. A bolt is anchored in the concrete by a collar (1) that expands as you tighten the nut above the mudsill (2).

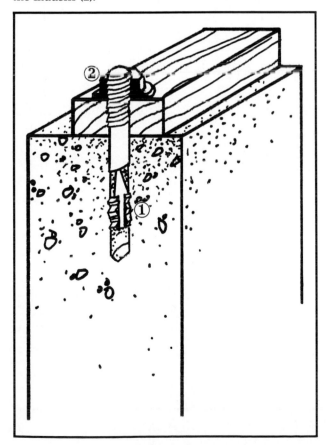

Retrofitting shear walls

Earthquakes can also exert considerable force against the connection between the house and the mudsill. The sill may be bolted to the foundation, but a house can still be thrown off the sill if it doesn't have a strong shear wall. A shear wall is a solid panel—preferably of ½-inch CDX plywood—that braces the connections between mudsill, studs and plate. New slab-foundation homes are usually built with ½-inch CDX plywood as sheathing and seldom need this retrofit. In many older homes, the only connection between the sill and the rest of the framing is 1-by-6 sheathing under exterior siding, which doesn't put up much of a fight in a quake.

If you've removed the exterior siding around the grade level of your house to do structural pest repairs, replace 1-by-6 sheathing with shear walls. If the siding is intact, retrofit the shear walls on the studs from the inside. You can use the same installation technique whether you retrofit from the inside or outside.

Shear walls give your home optimum protection when you install them all around the perimeter of the house. If you can't do a thorough retrofit because of time, cost or other obstacles, install the shear walls where they're most needed—at the corners. Shear walls should extend eight feet in each direction from substructure corners in a one-story house and sixteen feet in each direction in a two-story house. If you have a three-story house, they should run all around the substructure. You should also give a substructure wall full protection if both floor joists and roof rafters run parallel to it.

Cut the plywood to the proper length and height—it should fit from the base of the mudsill to the top of the plate—with a circular saw. Hold the panel in place and mark the positions of plate, studs, diagonal bracing and sill with chalklines. Tack the side nearest the corner with 10d common nails. Working from that side, nail the shear wall along the chalklines to every framing member behind it. Use 10d galvanized common nails and space them four inches apart, or use screws spaced six inches apart. A finished panel should be as tight as a drum across the studs.

Finally, drill ½-inch vent holes through the shear wall between each framing member. Drill one row close to the plate and another near the mudsill. This keeps moisture from building up behind the shear wall. After all this work, it won't do to have the retrofit undermined by a new fungus infection.

The substructure's framing will put up more resistance against seismic forces if it is retrofitted with a shear wall and blocking. The shear wall (1) is a ½-inch plywood panel that braces the mudsill (2), studs (3) and plate (4). The shear wall is nailed to the framing behind it with 10d galvanized nails spaced four inches apart (5). Vent holes (6) keep moisture from building up around the framing. Blocking (7) is made of 1⅛-inch plywood. The bottom edges are nailed to the shear wall and plates, and the top edges are fastened to the subfloor with Simpson L-90 reinforcing angles (8). Hurricane ties reinforce the connection between the blocking and the joists (9).

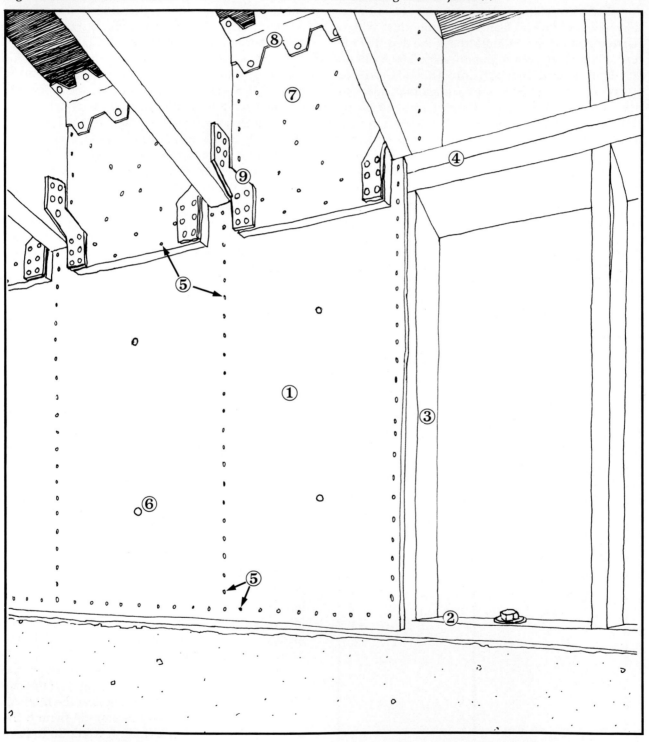

Blocking joists

In addition to securing the mudsill to the foundation and the stud wall framing to the mudsill, make sure that the joists are properly connected to the subfloor and stud wall. Ideally, wood blocking should be nailed in between the joists at the plates. There should be additional rows of blocking every 10 feet along the length of the joists. This blocking keeps the joists from tipping over in a major earthquake. The top edges of the blocking should be fastened to the subfloor and the bottom edges to the plates. This keeps the floor from separating from the substructure walls during an earthquake.

If your subfloor needs reinforcing, use 1⅛-inch plywood blocks the same length as the space between the joists and the same height as the joists. Toe-nail the ends of the blocking to the joists. At four-foot intervals, fasten the blocking to the subfloor with Simpson L-90 reinforcing angles. Attach them with #10 Phillips-head wood screws.

Blocking should be wider at the plates—the bottom should overlap the shear wall four inches when the top is flush against the subfloor. Nail the overlapping blocking to the shear wall and plate with 16d nails every three inches. Attach blocking to joists and subfloor as you did the rest.

Installing metal connectors

Besides connections in the substructure, earthquakes exert force against the connections between walls and the roof. These joints, however, are much harder to reach than those below the house. Gutters and roofing hide connections on the outside, and tight corners in the attic make these joints inaccessible from the inside. Most houses can only be retrofitted with connectors between roof and walls during an extensive remodeling or roofing job.

Whenever repairs expose the connection between rafters and the wall plates on which they rest, fasten them together with hurricane ties. Brace center girders with T-straps and L-straps.

If your house has more than one story, you can secure the framing on one level to the framing on another with pairs of hold-downs and threaded steel rods. Fasten one hold-down to the top of a stud in the first-floor wall and the other to the base of a stud directly overhead. Drill through the floor between them so you can link the two hold-downs with the threaded rod. You can also use hold-downs with anchor bolts in the substructure to fasten studs to the foundation.

Earthquake-resistant design is a very complex subject, and this chapter has only touched on the basics. As with structural pest control, design requirements vary from house to house. Homeowners and contractors often consult engineers before installing seismic retrofits. If you'd like to read more about the subject, consult the section on earthquake-resistant design in the bibliography.

Hurricane ties (1) are used to reinforce the connection between roof rafters and plates. L and T-straps (2, 3) strengthen the juncture between posts and girders. Hold-downs (4) can be used to tie the wall framing of one floor to the framing of another, and, in the substructure, to fasten studs to the foundation.

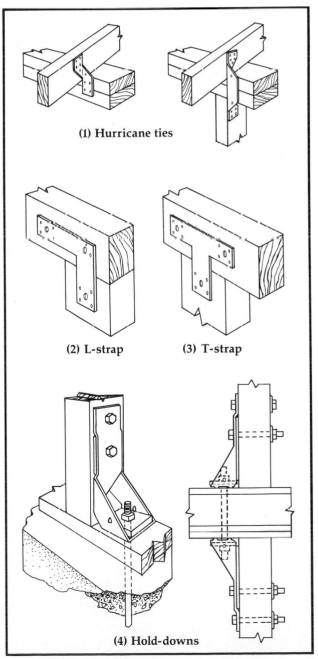

(1) Hurricane ties

(2) L-strap   (3) T-strap

(4) Hold-downs

Conclusion

The author hopes that this book helps you to make the right decisions about pest control work in your home. Ideally, it will help you to keep your home in such good shape that it never needs structural repairs.

The Termite Report distills a lot of experience with structural pest control, but it's certainly not the last word on the subject. It is an ongoing project. There's more to be discovered about pest-resistant home design. There's much more to learn from homeowners' experiences with pest control that will help lawmakers develop guidelines for the industry.

The author would like to hear about your experiences. What regulations do you think the pest control industry needs? What have you learned about maintaining your home? What have you learned about dealing with operators and realtors? Do you think we need a national organization to monitor the pest control industry and to research new methods of structural pest control? Should there be more state boards? Or would government regulations mess the situation up even more?

If you're interested in seeing some changes—in either this book or the pest control industry—please write to Pear Publishing, 1224 Lincoln Avenue, Alameda, California 94501.

Appendices

Bibliography

and

Index

Appendix I

The Symptoms of Pesticide Poisoning

Chlordane, heptachlor, lindane

All of these chemicals—in a single large dose or after repeated exposure—can cause fatal damage to the central nervous system, liver and kidneys. The lethal oral dose for a 150-pound adult in good health is one-fourth to one-eighth ounce (by weight) of pure pesticide, or twelve ounces (by volume) of diluted liquid. Symptoms of acute poisoning occur within 45 minutes of ingestion: excitability, irritability, disorientation or weakness, and sometimes nausea and vomiting. Convulsions may follow soon after. Finally, damage to the central nervous system may make breathing difficult and result in coma or death. Smaller doses might not cause immediate death, but would probably damage the liver and kidney.

Exposure to vapors may cause headache, nausea, vomiting, and irritation of eye, nose and throat membranes. Skin contact may also be harmful, since pesticides can be absorbed into the bloodstream through skin.

If an occupant shows the signs of acute poisoning, immediately phone the local poison control center or the emergency room of the nearest hospital, then phone your doctor. If the patient is alert and you have a poison safety kit on hand, you may be instructed to administer syrup of ipecac (which induces vomiting) followed by activated charcoal (which absorbs any poison remaining in the stomach). Keep the patient calm. If skin or hair is contaminated, bathe and shampoo vigorously with soap and water.

Pentachlorophenol

Pentachlorophenol, like other chlorinated hydrocarbons, damages kidneys, liver and the central nervous system. The lethal dose is about one-half ounce taken orally. Symptoms of acute poisoning include profuse sweating, headache, weakness, nausea and usually a fever. The patient may have a rapid heartbeat and pain in the chest and abdomen. Intense thirst, mental depression, stupor or convulsions may follow.

Pentachlorophenol is readily absorbed through skin. An occupant who has touched this chemical may have a rash in addition to the symptoms above. Exposure to vapors irritates the mucous membranes of the nose, throat and eyes.

In the case of acute poisoning, phone the local poison control center, hospital emergency room or your doctor. If the pentachlorophenol was swallowed, you may be instructed to give the patient syrup of ipecac, then activated charcoal. Bathe and shampoo contaminated skin and hair with soap and water. Reduce fever with a sponge bath, cold-water soaked towels or sheets.

Methyl bromide, sulfuryl flouride

A person in the vicinity of a house under fumigation may accidentally inhale vapors if wind blows the tarpaulin tent open or if, when the tent is removed, a gust blows residual gas in an unexpected direction. To prevent these accidents, observers should stand far back from the home. Neighbors within several hundred feet of the tented house should keep windows and doors facing the house closed.

Several breathfuls of a fumigant can kill. Fumigants (especially methyl bromide) penetrate skin, clothing, and even rubber gloves. Once a fumigant is released into the tent, no one should enter—not even to rescue a child or pet who is trapped or has wandered in—unless the rescuer has special gear. Otherwise, there will be more than one fatality.

Any known exposure to a fumigant, no matter how mild, should be treated as a medical emergency. Move patients to fresh air and have them sit or lie down and keep still. If the patient has difficulty breathing, give oxygen, mechanical artificial respiration or mouth-to-mouth resuscitation. Contact the local poison control center, hospital emergency room or your doctor.

In some cases, symptoms may be delayed for as long as 48 hours. People (especially children and pets) suspected of being exposed to a fumigant should be observed carefully for several days. Symptoms of mild exposure to fumigants include headache, dizziness, nausea and vomiting. Coughing of frothy sputum may mean that water is collecting in the lungs. Methyl bromide, in addition, irritates the membranes of the eyes, nose and throat. With severe exposure to a fumigant, the central nervous system may be injured. Symptoms in this case include drowsiness, tremors, muscle twitching and weakness. These may be followed by convulsions and coma. Death, if it occurs, is usually due to respiratory failure.

Appendix 2

Directory of State Agencies

Regulation of the structural pest control industry varies tremendously from state to state. Some states have virtually no problems with termites or beetles and have little need for specialized agencies. Some states are veritable zoos of structural pests and have established agencies specifically for the purpose of keeping firm control of operators, inspection reports and pesticide application. Other plagued states have chosen not to support separate bureaucracies for structural pest control.

If you live in California or in other states with structural pest control boards, you can usually depend upon these agencies to provide the legal standards and consumer support described in this book. If not, you need to be especially cautious when contracting operators. You cannot assume, for example, that state law holds operators liable for missed infestations. You can, however, write the conditions into your contract to purchase a home that will protect you from unexpected pest problems—for example, you might require the seller to order a complete inspection of the house and any attached structures.

In any case, you can familiarize yourself with the regulations pertinent to your situation by contacting one of the following state agencies. They will provide you with pamphlets or try to answer you personally.

Alabama
Department of Agriculture and Industries
Division of Plant Industry and Apiary
P.O. Box 3336
Montgomery, Alabama 36109
(205) 261-2650

Alaska
Division of Forestry
P.O. Box 7005
Anchorage, Alaska 99510
(907) 561-2020
or
Department of Labor
Mechanical Inspection
P.O. Box 7020
Anchorage, Alaska 99510

Arizona
Structural Pest Control Board
2207 South 48th Street, Suite M
Tempe, Arizona 85282
(602) 255-3664

Arkansas
State Plant Board
P.O. Box 1069
No. 1 Natural Resources Drive
Little Rock, Arkansas 72203

California
Structural Pest Control Board
1430 Howe Avenue
Sacramento, California 95825
(213) 620-2255 (in Los Angeles)
(415) 557-9114 (in San Francisco)
(916) 920-6323 (in Sacramento)

Colorado
Department of Agriculture
Division of Plant Industry
1525 Sherman Street
Denver, Colorado 80203
(303) 866-2838

Connecticut
Department of Environmental Protection
165 Capitol Avenue
Hartford, Connecticut 06106
(203) 566-5148

Delaware
Department of Agriculture
2320 South DuPont Highway
Dover, Delaware 19901
(302) 736-4811

District of Columbia
Office of Compliance
614 H Street, NW, Room 1107
Washington, DC 20001
(202) 727-7140

Florida
Department of Health and Rehabilitative Services
Office of Entomology
P.O. Box 210
Jacksonville, Florida 32231

Georgia
Department of Agriculture
Structural Pest Control Commission
19 Martin Luther King, Jr. Drive
Atlanta, Georgia 30334

Hawaii
Department of Commerce and Consumer Affairs
Pest Control Board
P.O. Box 3469
Honolulu, Hawaii 96801
(808) 548-2540

Idaho
Office of the Attorney General
Business Regulations Division
Statehouse
Boise, Idaho 83720
(208) 334-2400

Illinois
Attorney General
500 S. Second Street
Springfield, Illinois 62706
(217) 782-1090

Indiana
Deputy Attorney General
Consumer Protection Division
219 State House
Indianapolis, Indiana 46204
(317) 232-6330

Iowa
Department of Justice
Consumer Protection Division
Hoover Building, Second Floor
1300 East Walnut
Des Moines, Iowa 50319
(515) 281-5926

Kansas
State Board of Agriculture
Division of Plant Health
109 SW 9th Street
Topeka, Kansas 66612
(913) 296-2263

Kentucky
Office of the Attorney General
Capitol Building
Frankfort, Kentucky 40601
(502) 564-7600

Louisiana
Structural Pest Control Commission
P.O. Box 44153
Baton Rouge, Louisiana 70804

Maine
Department of Agriculture,
Food and Rural Resources
Board of Pesticides Control
Deering Building, State House Station 28
Augusta, Maine 04333
(207) 289-2731

Maryland
Department of Agriculture
Pesticide Applicators Law Section
50 Harry S. Truman Parkway
Annapolis, Maryland 21401
(301) 841-5710

Massachusetts
Department of Food and Agriculture
Pesticide Bureau
100 Cambridge Street, 21st Floor
Boston, Massachusetts 02202
(617) 727-7712 or 727-2863

Michigan
Department of Agriculture
Plant Industry Division
P.O. Box 30017
Lansing, Michigan 48909

Minnesota
Department of Agriculture
Agronomy Services Division
90 W. Plato Boulevard
Saint Paul, Minnesota 55107
(612) 297-2746

Mississippi
Office of the Attorney General
Consumer Protection Division
Carroll Gartin Justice Building
P.O. Box 220
Jackson, Mississippi 39205

Missouri
Department of Economic Development
P.O. Box 1157
Jefferson City, Missouri 65102

Montana
Department of Agriculture
Environmental Management Division
Agriculture/Livestock Building
Capitol Station
Helena, Montana 59620
(406) 444-2944

Nebraska
Department of Agriculture
Bureau of Plant Industry
P.O. Box 94756
Lincoln, Nebraska 68509
(402) 471-2394

Nevada
State Contractors Board
1800 Industrial Road
Las Vegas, Nevada 89158
(702) 385-0101

New Hampshire
Department of Agriculture
Pesticide Control Division
Caller Box 2042
Concord, New Hampshire 03301

New Jersey
Bureau of Pesticides Control
380 Scotch Road
West Trenton, New Jersey 08628
(609) 530-4122

New Mexico
Department of Agriculture
Bureau of Pesticide Management
P.O. Box 3AQ
Las Cruces, New Mexico 88003
(505) 646-2133

New York
Department of Environmental Conservation
Bureau of Pesticides Management
50 Wolf Road
Albany, New York 12233

North Carolina
Department of Agriculture
Structural Pest Control Division
P.O. Box 27647
Raleigh, North Carolina 27611

North Dakota
Attorney General
Consumer Fraud and Antitrust Division
State Capitol
Bismark, North Dakota 58505
(701) 224-3404

Ohio
Department of Agriculture
Pesticide Regulation
8995 E. Main Street
Reynoldsburg, Ohio 43068

Oklahoma
Department of Agriculture
Plant Industry Division
2800 N. Lincoln Boulevard
Oklahoma City, Oklahoma 73105

Oregon
Department of Agriculture
Plant Division
635 Capitol Street N.E.
Salem, Oregon 97310
(503) 378-3776

Pennsylvania
Bureau of Consumer Protection
Strawberry Square, 14th Floor
Harrisburg, Pennsylvania 17120
(717) 787-9707

Rhode Island
Consumer's Council
365 Broadway
Providence, Rhode Island 02902
(401) 277-2764

South Carolina
College of Agricultural Sciences
Department of Fertilizer and Pesticide Control
256 Poole Agricultural Center
Clemson University
Clemson, South Carolina 29634

South Dakota
Office of the Attorney General
Division of Consumer Affairs
State Capitol
Pierre, South Dakota 57501

Tennessee
Department of Agriculture
Division of Plant Industries
Ellington Agricultural Center
P.O. Box 40627, Melrose Station
Nashville, Tennessee 37204
(615) 360-0130

Texas
Structural Pest Control Board
1300 East Anderson Lane
Building C, Suite 250
Austin, Texas 78752
(512) 835-4066

Utah
Department of Business Regulation
Division of Contractors
Heber M. Wells Building
160 East 300 South
P.O. Box 45802
Salt Lake City, Utah 84145
(801) 530-6742

Vermont
Department of Agriculture
Plant Industry
116 State Street
Montpelier, Vermont 05602

Virginia
Department of Agriculture and Consumer Services
Division of Product and Industry Regulation
Office of Pesticide Regulation
P.O. Box 1163
Richmond, Virginia 23209

Washington
Department of Agriculture

West Virginia
Department of Agriculture
Plant Pest Control Division
Capitol Building
Charleston, West Virginia 25305
(304) 348-2212

Wisconsin
Department of Agriculture,
Trade and Consumer Protection
Agricultural Resource Management Division
801 West Badger Road
P.O. Box 8911
Madison, Wisconsin 53708
(608) 266-0197

Wyoming
Department of Agriculture
Consumer and Compliance Division
Cheyenne, Wyoming 82002
(307) 777-7321C

Appendix III Supplemental and Reinspection Reports

STANDARD STRUCTURAL PEST CONTROL INSPECTION REPORT

(WOOD-DESTROYING PESTS OR ORGANISMS)

This is an Inspection report only - not a Notice of Completion.

ADDRESS OF PROPERTY INSPECTED	BLDG. NO.	STREET	CITY	DATE OF INSPECTION
2001		Maple Street	Anytown CO. CODE 01	6-17-88

FIRM NAME AND ADDRESS
A-TERMITE Control
125 Main Street
Anytown, USA 00000-0000 (003) 555-7000

Affix stamp here on Board copy only

A LICENSED PEST CONTROL OPERATOR IS AN EXPERT IN HIS FIELD. ANY QUESTIONS RELATIVE TO THIS REPORT SHOULD BE REFERRED TO HIM.

FIRM LICENSE NO.	CO. REPORT NO. (if any)	STAMP NO.
1234		127990A

Inspection Ordered by (Name and Address) Sherry Nordstrom, Sure-Sale Realty 4000 Pleasant Dr., Anytown
Report Sent to (Name and Address) Sherry Nordstrom, Sure-Sale Realty 4000 Pleasant Dr., Anytown, USA
Owner's Name and Address Leah Cordova, 2001 Maple St., Anytown, USA
Name and Address of a Party in Interest Reliable Mortgage, 123 River St., Anytown, USA
Original Report ☐ Supplemental Report ☒ Limited Report ☐ Reinspection Report ☐ No. of Pages: 1

YES	CODE	SEE DIAGRAM BELOW	YES	CODE	SEE DIAGRAM BELOW	YES	CODE	SEE DIAGRAM BELOW	YES	CODE	SEE DIAGRAM BELOW
	S-Subterranean Termites			B-Beetles-Other Wood Pests			Z-Dampwood Termites		X	EM-Excessive Moisture Condition	
	K-Dry-Wood Termites			FG-Faulty Grade Levels			SL-Shower Leaks			IA-Inaccessible Areas	
	F-Fungus or Dry Rot			EC-Earth-wood Contacts			CD-Cellulose Debris			FI-Further Inspection Recom.	

1. SUBSTRUCTURE AREA (soil conditions, accessibility, etc.) -------
2. Was Stall Shower water tested? ------- Did floor coverings indicate leaks? -------
3. FOUNDATIONS (Type, Relation to Grade, etc.) -------
4. PORCHES . . . STEPS . . . PATIOS -------
5. VENTILATION (Amount, Relation to Grade, etc.) -------
6. ABUTMENTS . . . Stucco walls, columns, arches, etc. -------
7. ATTIC SPACES (accessibility, insulation, etc.) Accessible.
8. GARAGES (Type, accessibility, etc.) -------
9. OTHER -------

DIAGRAM AND EXPLANATION OF FINDINGS (This report is limited to structure or structures shown on diagram.)

General Description Wood frame, stucco side-wall/wood siding exterior, attached garage, occupied single family dwelling.
Inspection Tag Posted (location) Attic space.
Other Inspection Tags A-TERMITE Control 6-14-88.

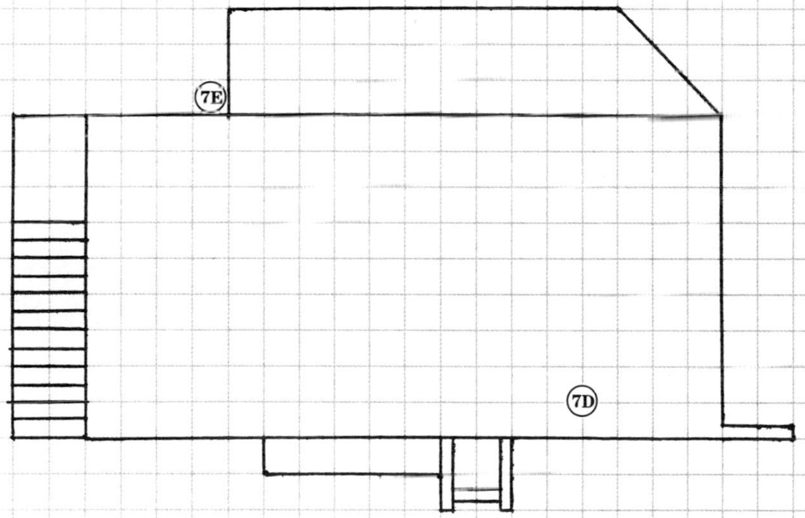

Per the California Structural Pest Control Act, Chapter 14, Section 8516, this report is considered to be a SUPPLEMENTAL REPORT. This report is at the request of the owner, Ms. Cordova. This report is intended to become part of and attached to A-TERMITE Control ORIGINAL REPORT, State Stamp No. 127986A, 6-14-88. This report is limited to the attic space area only.

ATTIC SPACE

7D Finding. (Information only) A small drywood termite infestation was observed in the wood support framing. The holes were covered with masking tape and re-checked. No evidence of an active drywood termite infestation was apparent. The wood members do not appear to have lost their ability to properly support the dwelling.

Rec. The owner is to periodically monitor this area for signs of an active infestation in the future. This report does not include repairs to the wood members/fumigation of the premises by A-TERMITE Control.

7E Finding. The moisture damaged corner area was opened for further inspection. Moisture damaged wood members were observed.

Rec. Remove the moisture damaged wood members and repair with new wood. Repair to match finish as close as possible.

Inspected by Michael Smith License No. AA 1234 Signature Michael Smith

YOU ARE ENTITLED TO OBTAIN COPIES OF ALL REPORTS AND COMPLETION NOTICES ON THIS PROPERTY FILED WITH THE BOARD DURING THE PRECEDING TWO YEARS UPON PAYMENT OF A $2.00 SEARCH FEE TO STRUCTURAL PEST CONTROL BOARD, 1430 HOWE AVENUE, SACRAMENTO, CA 95825.

STANDARD STRUCTURAL PEST CONTROL INSPECTION REPORT
(WOOD-DESTROYING PESTS OR ORGANISMS)
This is an inspection report only - not a Notice of Completion.

| ADDRESS OF PROPERTY INSPECTED | BLDG. NO. 2001 | STREET Maple Street | CITY Anytown / CO. CODE 01 | DATE OF INSPECTION 6-30-88 |

FIRM NAME AND ADDRESS
A-TERMITE Control
125 Main Street
Anytown, USA 00000-0000 (003) 55-7000

Affix stamp here on Board copy only
↓ **A LICENSED PEST CONTROL** ↓
↓ **OPERATOR IS AN EXPERT IN** ↓
HIS FIELD. ANY QUESTIONS RELATIVE TO THIS REPORT SHOULD BE REFERRED TO HIM.

FIRM LICENSE NO. 1234   CO. REPORT NO. (if any)   STAMP NO. 127999A

Inspection Ordered by (Name and Address) Sherry Nordstrom, Sure-Sale Realty 4000 Pleasant Dr., Anytown
Report Sent to (Name and Address) Sherry Nordstrom, Sure-Sale Realty 4000 Pleasant Dr., Anytown, USA
Owner's Name and Address   Leah Cordova, 2001 Maple St., Anytown, USA
Name and Address of a Party in Interest Reliable Mortgage, 123 River St., Anytown, USA
Original Report ☐ Supplemental Report ☐ Limited Report ☐ Reinspection Report ☒   No. of Pages: 1

YES	CODE	SEE DIAGRAM BELOW	YES	CODE	SEE DIAGRAM BELOW	YES	CODE	SEE DIAGRAM BELOW	YES	CODE	SEE DIAGRAM BELOW
	S	Subterranean Termites		B	Beetles-Other Wood Pests		Z	Dampwood Termites		EM	Excessive Moisture Condition
	K	Dry-Wood Termites		FG	Faulty Grade Levels		SL	Shower Leaks		IA	Inaccessible Areas
	F	Fungus or Dry Rot		EC	Earth-wood Contacts		CD	Cellulose Debris		FI	Further Inspection Recom.

1. SUBSTRUCTURE AREA (soil conditions, accessibility, etc.) Dry, accessible.
2. Was Stall Shower water tested? Yes.   Did floor coverings indicate leaks? No.
3. FOUNDATIONS (Type, Relation to Grade, etc.) Concrete, above grade.
4. PORCHES ... STEPS ... PATIOS Wood frame. No patio.
5. VENTILATION (Amount, Relation to Grade, etc.) Adequate.
6. ABUTMENTS ... Stucco walls, columns, arches, etc. Stucco exterior.
7. ATTIC SPACES (accessibility, insulation, etc.) Accessible.
8. GARAGES (Type, accessibility, etc.) Attached, accessible.
9. OTHER No other observations.

DIAGRAM AND EXPLANATION OF FINDINGS (This report is limited to structure or structures shown on diagram.)

General Description Wood frame, stucco side-wall/wood siding exterior, attached garage, occupied single family dwelling. Inspection Tag Posted (location) Subarea framing.
Other Inspection Tags Butler TERMITE Control 6-14-88.

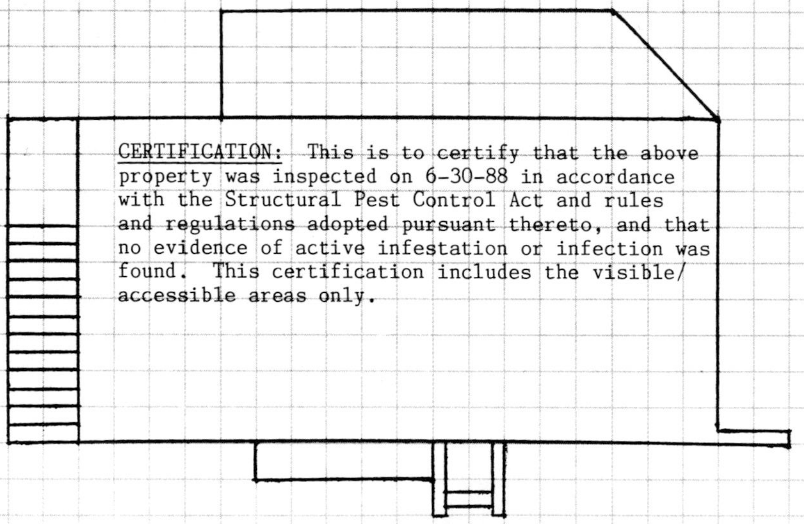

CERTIFICATION: This is to certify that the above property was inspected on 6-30-88 in accordance with the Structural Pest Control Act and rules and regulations adopted pursuant thereto, and that no evidence of active infestation or infection was found. This certification includes the visible/accessible areas only.

Per the California Structural Pest Control Act, Chapter 14, Section 8516, this report is considered to be a RE-INSPECTION REPORT. This report is intended to become part of and attached to A-TERMITE Control ORIGINAL REPORT, State Stamp No. 127986A, 6-14-88 and SUPPLEMENTAL REPORT, State Stamp No. 127990A, 6-17-88.

The following items outlined on A-TERMITE Control ORIGINAL REPORT, State Stamp No. 126986A, 6-14-88 and SUPPLEMENTAL REPORT,

6-17-88, have been completed by the owner.
ITEMS: 1A, 1B, 1C, 1D, 1E, 1F, 1G, 2B, 2C, 3A, 3B, 3C, 4A, 4B, 4C, 5A, 6A, 6B, 6C, 7A, 7B, 7C, 7E, 8A, 9A, 9B, 9C, 9D, and 9E.
ITEMS: 1A, 2A, and 7D are information only.

The owner has made repairs that are different than repairs recommended by A-TERMITE Control. No insect/wood destroying organisms are evident. Should interested parties require additional information about this item, the owner/local building department is to be consulted. No conditions conducive to insects/wood destroying organisms are evident in the visible/accessible areas. Interested parties are to clearly understand that A-TERMITE Control assumes no responsibility for work performed by others, and subsequently can offer no guarantees. A-TERMITE Control has no knowledge of chemical treatments. Should interested parties require additional information, the owner is to be consulted.

MEMBER PEST CONTROL ASSOCIATION

Inspected by Michael Smith   License No. AA 1234   Signature

Bibliography

Structural pest control

C.R. Coggins. *Decay of Timber in Buildings.* East Grinstead: Rentoleil Limited, 1980.

Charles A. Kofoid, ed. *Termites and Termite Control,* Berkeley: University of California Press, 1934.

Harry B. Moore. *Wood-Inhabiting Insects in Houses: Their Identification, Biology, Prevention and Control.* U.S. Department of Housing and Urban Development, 1979.

Charles S. Papp. *Introduction to North American Beetles.* Sacramento: Entomography Publications, 1984.

Arthur F. Verral and Terry L. Amburgey. *Prevention and Control of Decay in Homes.* U.S. Department of Housing and Urban Development, 1979.

W. Wayne Wilcox. "Wood: Decay During Use" in *Encyclopedia of Materials Science and Engineering,* Michael B. Bever, ed. New York: Pergamon Press, 1986.

W. Wayne Wilcox and David L. Wood. *So, You've Just Had a Structural Pest Control Inspection.* Berkeley: University of California Cooperative Extension, 1980.

Earthquake-resistant design

James Ambrose and Dimitry Vergun. *Seismic Design of Buildings.* New York: Wiley, 1985.

Norman B. Green. *Earthquake Resistant Building Design and Construction.* New York: Elsevier, 1987.

The Home Builder's Guide for Earthquake Design. Berkeley: Applied Technology Council with the U.S. Department of Housing and Urban Development, 1980.

Robert Iacopi. *Earthquake Country.* Menlo Park: Lane Publishing, 1981.

Index

S

Saddle cap, 100
Second opinion, 70
Seismic retrofits, 112, 120–123
  anchor bolts, 120–121
  blocking joists, 123
  brick foundation replacement, 120
  information sources on, 123
  metal connectors, 123
  shear walls, 121–122
Seller, inspection and repair concerns, 68–70
Shear walls, retrofitting, 121–122
Shelter tubes, 26, 27, 28
Shower leaks
  checking for, 41, 43, 44, 45, 46, 47
  repairing, 104–105
Siding
  checking, 32–33, 34, 48
  recommendations for, 48
Stairs, checking, 50, 51
Standard Notice of Work Completed and Not Completed, 52, 63
Standard Structural Pest Control Inspection Report, 52. *See also* Pest control report
State agencies, consumer complaint role of, 81
State laws
  inspection guidelines needed, 89
  liability for missed damage, 83
  pest control reports and, 52
  on pesticide use, 74, 86
State structural pest control boards, 9
Statute of limitation
  complaint filing caution, 63, 88
  frequency of inspection and, 83–84
Structural alterations, improper, 85
Structural defects, earthquake risks with, 110–119
Structural pest control boards, 9. *See also* California Structural Pest Control Board

Structural pest control inspection. *See* Pest control inspection
Structural pest control report. *See* Pest control report
Structural pests. *See* Pests
Structural safety, 7
  seismic retrofits for, 112, 120–123
Stucco house
  foundation capping for, *94*
  foundation curb for, 102
  inset gutters on, *114, 117*
  inspection problems with, 50
  rotted corners in, *48, 117*
  substructure decay in, *42, 62*
  workmanship concerns, 86
Stud wall, earthquake damage to, *118*
Substructure
  checking, 39–43
  repairing damage to, 41
  reports limited to, 71, 72, 82–83
  seismic retrofits in, 120–121, 123
Subterranean ground insertion, 75
Subterranean termites, 5, 25, 26, 27–28
  checking tree stumps for, 35
  evidence of, 32, 40
  inspection for, 27
  non-chemical options with, 77–79
  treatment for, 27–28, 75, 77–79
Sulfuryl flouride, 75, 76
Synthetic Pyrethroid, 28, 74, 75

T

Tent fumigation, 14, 75
  for beetles, 24
  double checking before, 76
  for termites, 28
Tenting. *See* Tent fumigation
Termite reports. *See* Pest control reports
Termites, 25–29
  distribution map, 25
  evolution of, 4
  non-chemical options with, 77–79

  swarm of, 24
  three types of, 5, 25. *See also specific types*
  treatment for, 74, 75
Toilet leaks, 44
  rebolting toilet for, 106–107
Tree stumps, 35, 43
"Trench and treat" method, 75
True powderpost beetles, 23–24
T-strap connectors, installing, 123

U, V

Unstable soil, earthquake safety concerns, 112
VA. *See* Veteran's Administration
Vegetation, as fungus source, 35
Vent holes, for plywood shear walls, 122
Ventilation
  checking in attic, 48
  checking in living areas, 46
  checking substructure for, 43
  preventive role of, 22, 35
Veteran's Administration (VA), as information source, 9

W

Walls. *See* Exterior walls
Wet rot, 5. *See also* Fungus damage
Wetwood termites. *See* Dampwood termites
White-rot fungi, evidence of, 22
Whittier, California, earthquake damage in, 110, *118*
Windows
  checking, 48
  problem areas in, *60*
  replacement quality concerns, 86, *87*
  replacing vs. repairing, 84–85
Wood preservatives, 22, 75